Parenting Apprenticeship:
YOUR CHILD'S CELEBRITY
Nurturing children through a new lens.

Eunice Essien

Cover illustrated by Temi Adedoyin

"Train up a child in the way he should go, and when he is old, he will not depart from it"

Kingdom Publishers

Copyright© Eunice Essien 2024

All rights reserved. No part of this book may be reproduced in any form by photocopying or any electronic or mechanical means, including information storage or retrieval systems, without permission in writing from both the copyright owner and the publisher of the book. The right of Eunice Essien to be identified as the author of this work has been asserted by her in accordance with the Copyright, Designs and Patents Act 1988 and any subsequent amendments thereto.
A catalogue record for this book is available from the British Library.

All Scripture Quotations have been taken from the New Kings James life application study Bible.

ISBN: 978-1-916801-07-3

1st Edition 2024 by Kingdom Publishers, London, UK.

You can purchase copies of this book from any leading bookstore or email
contact@kingdompublishers.co.uk

"Train up a child in the way he should go, and when he is old, he will not depart from it"

Dedication

To my beloved daughter Monique, my faith: You challenge me in every way possible to grow as a person and a parent, making me the mother that I have become today. I know that the principles of this book will inform your life, the nurturing of your own children and your children's children.

To my precious son Myron, my hope: Nurturing you has taught me the art of being an intentional committed mother making the principles of this book come to live as I allow myself to be nurtured to nurture. This book is not only dedicated to you but to your children and their children after them.

To my beloved mother, Cecilia Mensah: You are a dedicated mother. God bless you.

To every parent, parent-to-be, grand parents and guardians: May the principles of this book help you to create the foundation necessary for nurturing your child in the way he should go to bring you and your child peace and joy.

To my Partner, my heavenly Father and Friend: Without you this book would not have been possible. Thank you for the partnership. I look forward to more.

"Train up a child in the way he should go, and when he is old, he will not depart from it"

Some Scriptures that you may find helpful on this parenting journey. I have found them useful.

"Children are a heritage from the Lord; the fruit of the womb is a reward." – Psalm 127:3.

"Unless the Lord builds the house, they labour in vain who build it; unless the Lord guards the city, the watchman stays awake in vain." – Psalm 127:1.

"Fathers do not provoke your children to wrath, but bring them up in the training and admonition of the Lord." Ephesians 6:4.

"Train up a child in the way he should go, and when he is old, he will not depart from it." – Proverbs 22:6.

"Trust in the Lord with all your heart and lean not on your own understanding." – Proverbs 3:5

"There is a way that seems right to a man, but its end is the way of death." – Proverbs 16:25

"Many are the plans of a man's heart, but it is the Lord's purpose that will prevail." – Proverbs 19:21 (NIV).

"All things work together for good to those who love God, to those who are called according to His purpose." – Roman s 8:28.

"The Helper, the Spirit of truth will teach you all things and bring to your remembrance all that I have said to you." – John 14:26.

"Do not be conformed to this world, but be transformed by the renewing of your mind, that you may prove what is that good and acceptable and perfect will of God." – Romans 12:2.

"And whatever you do, do it heartily, as to the Lord and not to men, knowing that from the Lord you will receive the reward of inheritance for you serve the Lord Christ." – Colossians 3:23-24.

"The fruit of the Spirit is love joy peace patience kindness goodness faithfulness gentleness self-control." – Galatians 5:22-23.

> "Train up a child in the way he should go,
> and when he is old, he will not depart from it"

Hello

I'm delighted that you're reading this book. Whether you are a parent, grandparent, God-parent, guardian, parent-to-be or you have some kind of supervision of a child, reading this book will bless your life and your child's life.

> "Train up a child in the way he should go and when he grows, he will not depart from it." Proverbs 22:6

It's every parent's dream for their children to be good children and we set out as parents to do our best. I wanted to do good parenting. I set out to do my best as a parent. But when I messed up, I soon realised I was parenting with no strategy. I learned that good parenting does not happen by chance. It is intentional and deliberate. It requires proper planning and strategizing just like anything else that we intend to be successful at.

You want to succeed in your parenting?

Then read this book because you will learn ingredients and recipes that work. They have worked for me and have led me to the peace and joy I have in my life and in my relationship with my children. And so, I share them praying that whoever reads this book may be blessed.

One thing that I can assure you to learn from this book is that you will learn that 'train up a child in the way he should go,' goes beyond putting food on the table, buying nice clothes, toys and games, enrolling your child into the best schools, extra-curricular activities and all the other fancy things that money can buy.

"Train up a child in the way he should go,
and when he is old, he will not depart from it"

It goes beyond what you think the way for your child is. You have an idea or way that you have consciously or unconsciously mapped out for your child. I had my own idea. The problem with that was, I followed my own knowledge and understanding to formulate this way for my child. I did what I thought was 'normal'. Many parents are walking on the path that I did. You might be too. Then I had the revelation which changed this 'normal'; my beliefs, my thinking and attitude changed and I hope that as you read this book you may also have the revelation which will inform the nurturing of your children.

It does not matter what your religion, whether you are a Christian, Muslim, Hindu, Bahai, Sikh or whatever your religion is, the bottom line is you need God because we are all God's children. And in our lives today, the way for us to connect to God is through the Holy Spirit. God is a Spirit and if we are to relate to Him, we must do so spiritually. We can only connect and relate to Him through His own Spirit, Holy Spirit who through Jesus Christ dwells within us.

We all need the Holy Spirit to be able to connect to God in a way that God's intention, will and purpose for us and our children will be made known to us. Through this connection, you may be enlightened with God's intended way for your child and enable you to nurture him on that path.

I just want to put this out there, I am not talking about a quick fix situation, I am sharing about a journey; a life-long journey. It's a process of growth and fulfilment; of peace and joy. So be patient with yourself, your child and the process. Trust in God, knowing that He is working all things for your good.

I pray that as you read through *Parenting Apprenticeship: Your child's celebrity; nurturing children through a new lens*, you may be blessed in your own life, so that you may bless your child in the way he should go so that when he grows, he may not depart from it. God bless.

"Train up a child in the way he should go, and when he is old, he will not depart from it"

Contents

Chapter 1		15
You are a Celebrity.		15
Chapter 2		21
Your child's best interest		21
Chapter 3		27
The Partnership		27
Chapter 4		35
Water your child		35
Chapter 5		41
Your child's gift		41
Chapter 6		49
Parents		49
Chapter 7		59
Be Intentional in your parenting		59
Chapter 8		65
Create opportunity for nurturing		65
Chapter 9		71
Get yourself ready		71
Chapter 10		81
Behaviour Management		81
Chapter 11		91
Love Boundaries.		91

"Train up a child in the way he should go,
and when he is old, he will not depart from it"

Chapter 12	99
Nurtured to Nurture	99
Chapter 13	107
Wisdom	107
About Author.	119

"Train up a child in the way he should go,
and when he is old, he will not depart from it"

"Children are a heritage from the Lord;
the fruit of the womb is a reward." – Psalm 127:3

> "Train up a child in the way he should go,
> and when he is old, he will not depart from it"

Chapter 1
You are a Celebrity.

God created us in His image and likeness, and so we are His children. Let's look at what an image is. An **image** is a direct resemblance of an original and represents its nature or character. What does likeness mean? The word **likeness** means to look like, act like, and be like someone or something else. Therefore, as His children He created us to be in direct resemblance of Him, and that we will live, behave and be like Him in every essential way. But then we ate the forbidden fruit; sin entered the world and corrupted the holiness of God in us and distorted the image of God in us.

Ever since, as a loving Father, God's purpose and intent have been to restore us to our original holy nature. And that was why God sent His son Jesus Christ to the earth to live among us in the flesh, to show us what God is like; to teach us God's nature and character. And by His death on the cross, our sins will be covered making it possible for His image and holiness to be fully restored in us. And to be reconnected to our Father through His Holy Spirit.

Our parenthood parallels God's in that as physical beings and earthly parents, we birth our children in our image and likeness. It is very interesting and one that its implications should not be taken lightly. That means a parent is to reproduce the parent's nature in the child. A successful parent is one who successfully raises a child who essentially shares similar morals, ethical values and spiritual values as the parent. I suppose you want good morals, ethical values and spiritual values in your children. I want that. Do you?

You are a celebrity to your child. Right from day one your baby's looking up to you. Your baby wants to learn from you and be like you. You as a parent also consciously or unconsciously has the desires that somewhat meet your

> "Train up a child in the way he should go,
> and when he is old, he will not depart from it"

baby's needs. You want a mini 'you'. You look at the physical attributes of your baby and you ask, "Does my baby looks like me?"

No wonder when your child is old enough to walk, they begin to put on your clothes and shoes and make-up and behave like you. They even pretend to be like mummy or daddy in their demeanour and the way they speak. They imitate and copy you. Usually, parents laugh and feel entertained when little ones behave in this manner. I hope that from now on, as well as seeing the amusing side of this, you will begin to appreciate the inherent desire for your child wanting to be in your 'image and likeness'.

So right from day one, even before your child could say 'dada' or 'mama', you may be aware that your child had been copying you and learning from you. But the part that I want to draw your attention to is the fact that your child is not learning just your physical attributes or demeanour, they are learning and copying everything about you – physically, emotionally, spiritually, and morally. A typical example is we are told that when a baby senses anxiety or fear in his or her mother (or primary care giver), the baby picks up and mimics it in his or her behaviour. That is to say that for a mother who has episodes of anxiety, her baby may also display episodes of anxiety which may manifest in excessive crying or you may say the baby is unsettled.

Again, a baby can sense its parent's love or lack of it and thereby mimic that behaviour back in tensing or crying in the arms of the parent, just as the parent may display an uncomfortable demeanour around the baby.

So right from the get go, you are imparting your nature and character and behaviour in your child even before, they start to walk and talk. If you have noticed, from the above examples that I have given, what the baby picks from the parent are not tangible or material things but characteristics of the emotional state of the parent.

The point I am getting at is when it comes to raising our children, it is not about material things or the physical stuff. It is not about the shoes and the clothes, nor the expensive buggy or pram or the food on the table. I am not saying that these material things are not good, neither am I saying that they are not necessary. What I am saying is that, it is just the tip of the iceberg, a small part, so don't lose sight of the bigger colossal mass under the water. Many parents lose sight of what is underneath. I know I did.

Nurturing children is about raising godly children. When I was given the opportunity to learn this truth, it changed everything for me. Allow me to explain. Everything changed because suddenly I realised that I had been ignorant and so I have been neglectful of the needs – especially around spiritual and emotional of my children. How do I raise my daughter and my son to be godly? Am I godly? You may ask yourself the same questions and think about it for a minute before you continue.

The truth was, I didn't know what to do but what I did know was that I couldn't give what I didn't have. I couldn't teach what I didn't know. It is the same for you. You cannot give what you don't have neither can you teach what you don't know. And from that time on I made it my business to possess what I didn't have and what I didn't know. I devoted myself to learning. I am glad for you for buying this book because it tells me that you want to learn too. Not only do you want to do better you have taken the first step of acquiring knowledge. Good on you. I am delighted for you because you are on the right path. It is a good start indeed.

When I opened myself to learning, I also committed myself to change for the better. I opened myself to unlearning to relearn. There are people who learn some valuable things but they still remain in the same position. I did not want to be like that. I decided I was not only going to acquire knowledge but I was also going to practice what I learn or I am taught. I chose to become committed to intentional learning. In the process I developed a yearning and a learning heart. I became hungry and thirsty for learning: knowing the right thing and doing the right thing and the result was fulfilment as Matthew 5:6 says,

"Train up a child in the way he should go,
and when he is old, he will not depart from it"

"Blessed are those who hunger and thirst for righteousness, for they shall be filled."

The point I am trying to make is simple. If I want godly children then I must first be a godly parent. I wanted to become a godly parent who will raise godly children who will fulfil their life purposes and transfer their godliness onto their own children. I was looking into the future of not just my children but my children's children. It opened my eyes to a worthwhile legacy. A legacy that is not material based. A legacy that is perpetual. It became my new definition of success for me when it comes to parenthood.

I realised that successful parent to God, is not about achieving A in mathematics or going to the best school or the best holiday or eating the most expensive food or wearing the best clothes money can buy, but raising children who share in the moral, ethical and spiritual values of the parent; children who will live, worship and serve the Lord through their lives and bless others.

Working on my character for good then shaped my behaviour and attitude. I became positive and nurturing. It was hard for me because my daughter was a teenager and my son was pre-teen. The good news for you is, your case is different. You may have a baby or younger child who may still be in their formative years. Take this opportunity to sort yourself out. Sort your character out. You want good children. Are you good yourself? It is nearly impossible to train good and godly children when you as a parent has a bad character. You know the saying, "The apple does not fall far from the tree."

You can only give what you have. Can you imagine telling a child to be honest and all you do is tell lies around your child. You receive a phone call and because you do not want to speak with the person on the line you tell your spouse to tell them you are not home. Meanwhile your child is sitting right next to you watching and listening to you. You keep telling your little child that you would do something for him and yet you don't follow through and go ahead to yell at him when he reminds you, just because he reminded you a couple of minutes ago. Soon enough your child will learn to tell lies. And the

> "Train up a child in the way he should go,
> and when he is old, he will not depart from it"

day you discover that he has been lying to you, you'd become angry and probably yell, 'Don't lie to me, I always teach you to tell the truth, and now you are lying to my face'. Really…

The truth is, you have been telling him one thing but your behaviour is also telling him another. Your young child may be thinking to himself, 'If it's so important to be honest then why is mummy or daddy not honest?' And since children learn predominantly by watching, they learn your lying behaviour rather than your words. Your child gives you back your own behaviour. He mirrors your character to you and you can't handle it. Remember your child wants to be like you.

You are a celebrity…

Never forget that.

"Train up a child in the way he should go,
and when he is old, he will not depart from it"

Take a moment to Reflect:

In what ways do you see your child copying or imitating you?

From what you have read from this chapter, reflect on what you have learned to inform your nurturing of your child as the 'celebrity' that you are?

Pray for yourself and your child.

*"Train up a child in the way he should go,
and when he is old, he will not depart from it"*

Chapter 2
Your child's best interest

Now you know you are a celebrity whose moves are being watched 24/7 by your child. Not just watching you but you are imparting your child's life physically, emotionally and spiritually with every move and decision you make. How does that make you feel? I will tell you how it made me feel when I realised this for myself. It opened my eyes and I felt important but also scared. Important because I am blessed to be a celebrity with two fans (I have two children) and that I have someone looking up to me. It scared me because of the realisation that privilege placed on my life; the responsibility to shape my children's life. The magnitude of the responsibility made me want to do a good job. When I say a good job I mean, do my best and not settle for average or mediocrity.

I realised that the kind of celebrity I wanted to be could not be achieved by doing things anyhow. I couldn't do it by chance. That kind of success required planning, strategy and being intentional and deliberate in my behaviour, and relationship with my children. I felt privileged and worthy not because I am better than others. No. I realised that I was chosen to be a parent for a purpose. To be specific, I was chosen to be mother to my children for a purpose. And guess what? God considered me worthy and the perfect person for my children. God trusted me with my children who also belong to God. Not that I deserved it but He did it for a purpose. That means a lot.

He knew I am a good person and I am a good celebrity for my child. The problem was, I had my babies without this in-depth knowledge of who I was and still am in God's eyes. And so, once I had my babies, I did my own thing. Right from day one I set off on my own orchestrated road without knowledge, understanding and wisdom. I did what I thought was right.

> "Train up a child in the way he should go,
> and when he is old, he will not depart from it"

Everyone was doing it, so it must be right and normal. I was ignorant of the trust and the magnitude of the responsibility that God has placed on me.

The point is when God chose me as a mother for my child, He knew the road that He had set before me. He knew being a parent is a great joy but it is also a huge responsibility – one that He did not require me to do it solo. He knew I couldn't be successful on my own because He knew it is a broken world; it's a scary world… Besides He has the wisdom of how to nurture my child to become the best. He called me a parent, a mother so that He will be in partnership with me to nurture my child in the way he or she should go.

It is the same for you. You are precious to God. He loves you and He wants you to do a good job. The point is He has not wired you to do it solo. For you to be successful you have to partner with Him. He knows the purpose for bringing your child to this earth. He knows what He wants your child to do here. Your child is here on a mission. You don't fully know. Neither do you fully understand. It's therefore in your best interest and in your child's best interest that you partner with Him who fully knows and fully understands and can fully lead you there successfully.

It brings me joy that you are gleaning some nuggets now to set your child on a good foundation whilst your child is still little. I learned the hard way because I did not have the opportunity to read a book like this. Someone sharing their story with me; sharing some ingredients and recipe with me. And so, I messed up and I don't want the same for you. It is harder to undo a mess to redo the right than getting it right from the start.

My dear celebrity parent, it is time for you to sort yourself out. It is time to work on yourself and get yourself in position. You may have taken your parenting responsibility for granted. I am not talking in terms of the 'tip-of-the-iceberg' provision for your child. I am talking in terms of the totality of the iceberg (tip, middle and what lies at the bottom of the water); physical, emotional, spiritual provision. The question then is how do you partner with God? How do you work together on this journey?

"Train up a child in the way he should go, and when he is old, he will not depart from it"

I will deal with this in the next chapter. But for now, I want to focus on something that I had to deal with within myself to build a foundation that grounded me in order to progress on my journey of nurturing my children. It is just as important for you too. It's your motivation.

Your motivation

I can give you all the guidance and advice under the sun for nurturing your precious child, however it may soon become a check list for you. Check lists lose their appeal eventually because they are shallow and lack depth. It becomes repetitive and boring. And so, you'll soon give up on them. With the right motivation and attitude, guidance and encouragement become more attractive, meaningful and persist for longer. Depending on the kind of motivation and level of commitment, you will find that the guidance in this book for nurturing your child may be longer lasting if not a life time. UNLESS YOU HAVE THE RIGHT FOUNDATION... FORGET IT...

Be honest with yourself and reflect. I had to do it at some point in my parenting journey; about 6 years ago. I had a teenager and a preteen at the time and parenting was a tedious and difficult task. As a parent I was doing the best that I thought. And my motivation was coming from the fact that I wanted my children to appreciate me for what I did for them and so they would respect me and do as I say. I also wanted people to see that I was a good mother for doing a good job with my children.

Appreciation and respect from your child and others seeing the good job you do with your child are good things, if they do happen. But as sources of motivations, they are bad ones. No wonder, I became so frustrated when I was not getting the level of appreciation and respect that I had envisioned and it impacted on my relationship with my children. And no wonder I became so fearful of what people thought of me.

I was looking for external approval and appreciation of what I was doing. Did I appreciate myself for the things I did for my children? NO! Did I receive

"Train up a child in the way he should go,
and when he is old, he will not depart from it"

the appreciation that God was giving me? NO! Why? Because I had no idea. I was looking at and expecting from the wrong sources. You may share the same motivation as I did years ago. Here is your chance to rethink.

When I decided to lean on God after I discovered my identity, my motivation changed. I realised that my "children are a heritage of God" (Psalm 127:3), and that my children belong to God. I am therefore accountable to Him – not people. As children grow in years, parents' tight grip is supposed to loosen to predominantly be that of a guide. It was then I realised that if I did not have a meaningful relationship with my children, I couldn't be a guide. I would lose that role and guess what? I am accountable to God.

Therefore, being a mother and nurturing my children has nothing to do with appreciation from my children or people. I was doing it for God. It made sense when I realised that anything and everything I did and do, I am doing it onto God. And the appreciation and reward from God is even better. I want God to look at me and say,

"Eunice, my child, you are a good and faithful servant. I gave you 2 children and you have done a marvellous job. Come to me and here is your reward".

This became my motivation and it still is. Suddenly my motivation has changed from a selfish myopic one to a meaningful one and one that has roots in my source – God. This is peaceful and fulfilling and hopeful. Whatever I do to nurture my children I am not doing it because I am looking for something in return from them. They don't owe me. And I am not doing them a favour by nurturing them.

I love my children because they are my children but more importantly, I love them because I love God. The love I have for my children is made meaningful through the love I have for God. In other words, the love I have for them is based on my love for God. I pray that I set a good example for them so that they may also be good example for their own children. In truth, I see it as a blessing to have the opportunity to be a mother to two perfect

> "Train up a child in the way he should go,
> and when he is old, he will not depart from it"

gifts. I value my relationship with my children and so I am intentional about nurturing it.

You may have some thinking of your own to do. Start right or make amendments now whilst your child is still a young.

"Train up a child in the way he should go,
and when he is old, he will not depart from it"

Take a moment to reflect:

What is your motivation?

Are you looking for appreciation from your child?

Are you looking for appreciation from people?

Take a few minutes to reflect and if you have a journal put your thoughts in journal.

Pray and ask God to help and direct you.

"Train up a child in the way he should go, and when he is old, he will not depart from it"

Chapter 3
The Partnership

I'm hoping that so far you see my point of you being a celebrity and the fact that it is in your interest and your child's best interest to partner with God who gave you your child so that you may be able to nurture your child in the *WAY* he should go, not your way but God's *WAY*. Your way may seem right to you but it may lead to destruction as highlighted by Proverbs 16:25:

"There is a way that seems right to a man, but its end in the way of death."

As I pointed out earlier, the question then is how do you partner with God? How do you work together on this journey? It is through your relationship with Him; through allowing him to nurture you to nurture your child; through developing and growing your character.

Your relationship with Him

I have come to the observation that the one single most important relationship you may want to keep, cultivate and nurture is your relationship with God. Everything you need is in God. You may say, "I go to church." Yes, going to church is good but I am not talking about going to church or engaging in some religious activities. I am talking about a personal meaningful relationship like you would have with a friend. The more you keep in touch with your friend, talking and spending time together, the closer and intimate you become sharing feelings and thoughts. You get to know what is on their minds and in their hearts because they tell or share with you and you do the same. That is the kind of relationship God created you to have with Him.

*"Train up a child in the way he should go,
and when he is old, he will not depart from it"*

The only person who is able to connect you to this level of closeness and intimacy with God is the Holy Spirit. You need that personal relationship with Him to thrive and bear fruits. "If you abide in me and I in you, you will bear much fruits" John 15:5. Through your spending time with God in prayer, reading his word, and reflecting on them, you become transformed by the Holy Spirit who enables the renewing of your mindset to know the things that are good, pleasing, and perfect will of God for your life and that of your child (Romans 12:2).

It starts with recognising and accepting that:

> *"Unless the Lord builds the house, they labour in vain who builds it; unless the Lord guards the city, the watchman stays awake in vain" – Psalm 127:1.*

This simply means that you cannot achieve the best you want by yourself. You may try but you may just hurt yourself and your child in the process. No wonder there is so much pain and stress in our homes and our relationships. It is because we are doing it all by ourselves. And we don't have to. And that, is the good news.

When I had this revelation, I became hungry and thirsty for this connection and the more I read and reflected on the words and prayed I felt closer to God. And I wanted more and more of that closeness and He also got closer to me and our connection became stronger through the Holy Spirit. So, that the Holy Spirit could direct me to the intentions and will of God for my children and I.

This connection of the Holy Spirit is one single most important ingredient when it comes to nurturing my children and living my life. I receive knowledge, understanding and wisdom with which I live my life and to be a godly parent to my children (a godly celebrity). He teaches me things I don't know and even reminds me when I forget. It is amazing. Jesus Christ emphasised this connection in John 14:26,

> "Train up a child in the way he should go,
> and when he is old, he will not depart from it"

"The Helper, the Spirit of truth will teach you all things and bring to your remembrance all that I have said to you."

Allow yourself to be nurtured to nurture your child

Allowing yourself to be nurtured comes from the concept of apprenticeship – a revelation I received some years back when I was so frustrated and stressed with life and parenting. God explained to me that I am a parent who is learning on the job just as apprentices do. The question was, "Who was I learning from and who was teaching me the job of parenting?" God gave me the job to be a parent and so He has employed me with no prior experience. And as an apprentice, I must learn from Him because He knows the job for which He has employed me. It is the same for you.

You want the best for your child. He also wants the best or your child. He fully knows what is best for your child and how to get it and so it makes sense to learn from Him. And that is what I did. That is why I allow myself to be connected to God through the Holy Spirit so that I can learn how to be a godly parent and how to deliver godly parenting to my child so that what is best for my children may manifest. It is every hour, every day, every week, every month every year relationship that direct the nurturing of my life and my children. I learn a lot about myself whilst I nurture my children, it's amazing. I go to God with practically anything. Here are a few examples:

- I remember I went to God one morning telling Him, "My child does not want to go to school today, I cannot get through him, what is going on Lord?" He tells me, "Leave it to Me." And within 20mins, he was all dressed up ready for school without me saying another word.
- "My child told a lie and I can't get him to admit it, what shall I do?" He tells me, "Be patient and be compassionate. What can you learn here?" And He reminds of a Bible story that enables me to learn.

"Train up a child in the way he should go,
and when he is old, he will not depart from it"

- "I am upset with my child's behaviour, what shall I do?" He may tell me, "Be Patient, how is your own behaviour?" I became intentional about my own behaviour, became disciplined. God used this to nurture my own character and I felt so much peace. My child copied my actions.
- "I am getting upset that my child is not cleaning up after herself in the bathroom although I have prompted her a few times with no good results. What shall I do?" He tells me, "Don't be angry or frustrated. Do it yourself and be grateful for having hands and legs and strength to do the cleaning." I obeyed and I felt at peace. And after a while, she started cleaning up after herself with no arguments.
- "My children don't want to come to church with me and I want them to because I know it is good for them." He tells me "Don't force them, leave it to me."
- "My young adult is going somewhere and I don't agree for her to go. Now she is asking for money from me to enable her go." He tells me "Give her the money. I will watch over her. Don't worry." Not only did I give her the money, I went an extra mile; I dropped her off when she requested. And it felt so good, my peace returned to me.
- "I don't like the kind of friends my child is moving around and spending time with. He tells me, "Love them, love them all."

There are no surprises for God because He knows even before I go to Him. And each time when I follow through with what He directs, I find peace and eventually good results follows. I find peace because my perspective changes and I move from seeing things through my own human eyes to seeing things through the eyes of God. And then it brings peace and joy to my spirit, my soul and by physical being. Allowing myself to be nurtured to nurture is learning to trust and obey God even when I don't understand. One thing I always enjoy is the peace and joy even in the moment of doing something that I would not ordinarily have done. Try it!

> "Train up a child in the way he should go, and when he is old, he will not depart from it"

Developing and growing your character

Character is something I talk about all the time because it is so important. It takes a long time to develop and grow character. Why? It is an inside job. It grows from within and then it comes out. And as human beings, culture, traditions and customs and distortions have programmed us to live from the outside in. And this way of living makes us incongruent or hypocrites because what goes on within us is different from what we display outside. That's why we have fake people. They say one thing in the morning and they say another thing in the afternoon. Or someone may tell you "I love you" but inwardly he or she is cursing you.

And as you are a celebrity to your child, training up your child in the way he should go, it is important that you pay attention to character. Yours and that of your child and be intentional about it. These things do not happen by chance. If you remember from earlier, I did mention the fact that we are created in the image and likeness of God. Therefore, when we want to know and grow our true character, we have to look at the nature and character of God. God is love. The character of God is:

LOVE	PATIENCE	FAITHFULNESS
JOY	KINDNESS	GENTLENESS
PEACE	GOODNESS	SELF-CONTROL

It's easier to model character for your child. It's easier to show them with your actions than using words. Using both words and actions that match your words is the way to go. That is what I do. I'll share an example with you.

I have become intentional about reaching out to do good and be kind to others. I usually cook fried rice once a week or every other week. Well... whenever I do cook the fried rice, I give some to my neighbours to bless them. I don't make a lot but I make enough to give them at least a plate each. My son sees me do this from time to time. He just looks on with admiration.

> "Train up a child in the way he should go,
> and when he is old, he will not depart from it"

One time I decided to drop a plate to a neighbour who lived about 15 minutes' drive away. On this occasion my son had just come back from school and was helping himself to some snacks.

So, after I dropped the plate for the next-door neighbour, my son saw me with another plate and he was surprised and asked, "Who is this one for?" And as I explained it was for the neighbour living 15minutes' drive away, he was just thrilled and delighted as he said, "Wow mummy that is really nice." He immediately offered me some of his snack, "Mummy, have some of my biscuit. I want to share with you." I really didn't want a biscuit but I took one and ate it.

My heart was overjoyed, it was beautiful. Then I felt within my spirit, the Holy Spirit telling me, "You are bearing some good fruits and sowing seeds in your child." Then I prayed, "God water this seed and when the time is right let the fruits show in my son to bless others and bring glory to me. My glory is Your glory."

A week later, he comes home from school and I could tell there was something he wanted to tell me. He was so excited, "You won't believe what happened, mummy?" "What happened?" I asked. "I bought lunch for a friend at school today. He did not have money to buy food and so I paid for his lunch." "That's kind of you, how do you feel?" "It feels great." "It is loving yourself and loving others. It's amazing, isn't it? Now, you know how I feel when I drop those plates of fried rice to the neighbours." He just beamed with smiles and just gave me a hug.

Then the Holy Spirit reminded me of something. A couple of days prior to this, he'd called me after school and asked for some money for food. He actually asked for enough money to buy for himself and for a friend. I remember grabbing my laptop, went to online banking and put some money into his account. Oh my God, I realised that as I am modelling the character of goodness and kindness to my son in my own little way in my everyday life, it is taking root in his own character too. After all, I am his celebrity!

> "Train up a child in the way he should go, and when he is old, he will not depart from it"

And since you are a celebrity to your child, I hope you see why it is important to grow your character and the example I have given above may help you to come out with some ideas of your own. I always say, "Be intentional about it."

In my relationship with God, I see God as my CEO, Jesus Christ as my Manager and the Holy Spirit as my Supervisor.

God bless.

"Train up a child in the way he should go,
and when he is old, he will not depart from it"

Take a moment and reflect:

What is your relationship with God like? Are you connected to God in a personal relationship?

Who have you been learning from and how are you getting on so far?

What are your thoughts and allowing yourself to be nurtured to nurture?

Review the 9 characters and think of your own ways that you may model it for your child?

Pray and ask God to help and direct you.

> "Train up a child in the way he should go,
> and when he is old, he will not depart from it"

Chapter 4
Water your child

I got it wrong. I did not get it right from the beginning. I had to learn the hard way but grace has intervened and I live to enjoy peace and hope and joy in my life, my home and in my relationship with my children. I am therefore delighted that I have been blessed with the opportunity to share with you, first to create awareness, to cause you to decide to change for the better and choose to follow it through and finally for you to enjoy the peace and joy and hope in your relationships with your child and your family at large.

I recall to memory when I was a little girl growing up. From as long as I can remember, my mum was a frustrated woman, wife and mother. In fact, her children were not the problem at all but through her frustrations she would run her mouth with negative words on her children. My dad was a strict silent disciplinarian. He could wage cold wars for years, I'm told. Thank God that was not my experience of him.

I am one of the younger ones, the 9th of 10 children, and so although his cold wars were not my experience, I had my own version of his strictness and intimidation as a parent. But there was another side to my dad that I experienced, a fun side that I enjoyed. He would gather my young twin siblings, my young nephew and I around and told us folklore stories. Some of these stories contained songs, and believe me, he sang them all. We just sat enjoying ourselves in those moments. It was pretty good. More of this and less intimidation from him would have been wonderful.

As I was saying, my mum was good with her mouth and her words when it came to negative words – insults and curses. She was an expert at scolding you from head to toe. My mum loved us but not in so many words. However, when I did something which she considered to be wrong, she was like a poet

> "Train up a child in the way he should go,
> and when he is old, he will not depart from it"

or a novelist. She employed figurative language, imageries, similes, personifications, metaphors, you name it; she used them all; to rain those negative words. She was like an African version of Shakespeare. I could actually picture vividly in my mind's eye all the imageries she was using. That was how good she was. She was and is still very articulate in her literary devices. Except that she doesn't use those negative words on her children any more. She blesses us more.

My mum has since apologised and I can tell that she is very much sorry for her behaviour all those years ago. I realise that her life circumstances were difficult for her and so she took her frustrations on her children. Whilst I understand why she behaved in that manner and I forgive her, what she did was wrong. It was not good nurturing. Actions have consequences. And one thing I want to make clear is even if you have reason for doing something wrong, more often than not, it does not stop the consequences of your actions or choice from happening.

Some of you may have similar experience with your own parents. It is a blessing and by grace that some of us have turned out the way we have.

As a child and a teenager, I did not like the way she rained those negative words on me and my siblings however, I guess over the years, I got used to them. I mean, you do. They become normal.

Then I grew older, then I had a baby. I became a mother. Then my baby became mobile; crawling going everywhere and anywhere. My child started touching everything and then the temper tantrums followed. Before I knew it, I was running my mouth. I was not as good as my mum, that's for sure but I was running my mouth with negative words. I did not mean to intentionally do that, but I found myself using negative words. It started little by little.

First it was simple, NO! STOP IT, KEEP QUIET, YOU ARE NAUGHTY. By the time I realised I was streaming negative sentences. Sentences became paragraphs. When the words of the parents are negative, the home environment becomes negative and soon enough the child's attitude also becomes negative. With both parents having negative attitude and using words that tear down instead of building; and harsh criticisms, those words manifest in your child's behaviour and attitude as he or she gets older. The consequence of that was I ended up stripping my child off her confidence. I ended up with a with an anxious child. I didn't know what I was doing until it was done.

When I became a mother, I wanted the best for my child. My child was good and perfect because God gave me a good and perfect gift. So how did I end up with an anxious child? How did I end up ruining my child instead of building her up? Was that the best for my child? Of course not. Let me tell you something about negative words. Negative words destroy. Proverbs 18:21 says

> *'Death and life are in the power of the tongue and those who love it will eat its fruits'*

Let's talk about the tongue... the tongue is powerful. God spoke the world into being and since we are made in the image of God and likeness, we have that power too. We can create or we can destroy with our mouth; our words. Negative words are death and positive words are life. As a parent of a young child, mind the things you say with your mouth to your child. We are in a system where there seem to be no time. Parents are rushed off their feet, working long hours and sometimes end up bringing work home. They are stressed and frustrated. Perfect conditions for negative words. You take your stress and frustration on your poor child when he or she 'misbehaves' or does not do as you expect them. You shout and run your mouth at your child who is only being a child.

For some of you, as little as your child is, just because he or she touched something you did not want them to or kept you on your toes for a little, you call them "Trouble". Then you wonder why they become trouble for you. It starts as joke but it has its implications because the tongue is powerful. So be

> "Train up a child in the way he should go,
> and when he is old, he will not depart from it"

mindful of your words. If you are in the habit of calling your child negative words...a word to the wise is enough.

Water your child to life with positive words. You want your child to grow, blossom and flourish, so give them the water they need. Even when your child does something that you consider to be wrong or mistakes, be intentional to find a way to water them with positive words. The point is when you look for something good in your child, you will find it.

One night during our usual bed time conversations, my son brought up something that was on his mind. "Mum," he said. "Yes LD", I responded. "Am I naughty?" he continued with a concerned face. I could tell he was sad. I looked at him and asked him, "What makes you say that?" "I did some things wrong today but even then; you just love me and you are so kind to me" was his explanation. He was just puzzled that even when he did things wrong, I just loved and cared for him. Not only was he remorseful for what he did, but he appreciated the love and kindness from me.

With consideration and understanding I reassured him, "Aw, I agree with you that you did some things wrong. You made some bad choices today and so the behaviour that followed was naughty. But you on the other hand, are good. You are blessed and you are awesome. Never forget that. I am so blessed that God chose me to be your mother. I love you so much." You should see the light that suddenly glowed in his eyes. It was amazing. With that he said, "I love you too mum and I am sorry." And we both enjoyed the hug that followed.

When your child is old enough to understand some basic things as part of growing up, he knows when he has done something wrong. By all means rebuke the bad behaviour in a calm and sensitive manner – I mean without losing your cool. The last thing he needs is for you raining your words. He just needs love, compassion, comfort and reassurance. And when you are able to do that, you are watering your child with good stuff. Moving away from using negative words require time and patience with yourself too. It requires a character change because behaviour is rooted in character.

If you go to attack the behaviour without a character change, the behaviour might die down only for a short time because the foundation of that behaviour has not been dealt with. It's like a tree. When you cut off the leaves because it does not look nice, in no time the same leaves will reappear again because the roots of the not-nice-leaves are still active. Behaviour has to be dealt with at source – character

As a parent you must realise that God has given you good and perfect gifts (James 1:17). If I have not mentioned this before, let me say it now, your child is a gift from God. Your child is good. It is your responsibility to nurture this goodness in them. What best way to do it than watering them with your kind and loving words. Rebuke behaviour and choices that are unwise or not considerate but build your child up with positive words so that they will receive the nourishments to blossom. Water your child with your words. It is that simple.

It is simple but not always easy especially when your settings are set at negative words. In other words, it is not easy when you are so used to raining your mouth with negative words. Having said that you can do it because…you can! But remember to do it with the strength from the Holy Spirit asking Him to remind you. And then be intentional and little by little you will develop positive words as your negative words decreases. It's like muscle. You develop muscles when you burn out fat.

> Water your child with your positive words. Look at your child and focus on "whatever is true, whatever is noble, whatever is just, whatever is pure, whatever is lovely, whatever is good…and whatever is praiseworthy" (Philippians 4:8). If anything is admirable and praiseworthy that is what you put your attention on and to water your child.

"Train up a child in the way he should go,
and when he is old, he will not depart from it"

Take a moment to reflect:

What is your experience as a child with your parents. Did they use negative words or positive word?

How did you feel then as a child?

Now as a parent, assess your words, are they positive or negative?

From what you have learned from this chapter what can you do differently?

"Train up a child in the way he should go, and when he is old, he will not depart from it"

Chapter 5
Your child's gift

Your baby is pure and innocent and beautiful. If you remember from earlier, I have talked about the fact that your child is a gift from God. And God only gives good and perfect gifts. God has also deposited good and perfect gifts in your child. Just as your child, your child's gifts are pure, innocent and beautiful. And as to whether the purity, innocence and beauty of your child's gifts grow and develop, depend on how you nurture your child.

Are you doing your own thing? Or are you allowing yourself to be nurtured to nurture your child? Are you leaning on your own wisdom or you are leaning on God's wisdom? How do you learn from God? We have already established that it is through your relationship with Him (Chapter 3). And through that relationship you may obtain the wisdom to nurture the purity and beauty of your child's gifts. Leaning on the wisdom of God is my secret to nurturing my child. Well…like a lot of things, I did not get this right from the start and I made a mess of things. But there came a time when I had to question who I was learning from and that was when I learned the power from my source – God.

So be glad that you get to share in things that I had to learn directly from God. That you may be blessed whilst you still have a baby or a child in primary school. And even though my daughter is a very young adult, and my son is a teenager, my secret is still God. I usually say that I am blessed to know the Best and I learn from the Best. I will not have it any other way because God gives me the secure foundation. And building on this foundation, here is something for your tool kit. It sounds like I'm teaching, right? …well, yeah, I am teaching LOL. Here we go…

"Train up a child in the way he should go,
and when he is old, he will not depart from it"

Encourage your child's curiosity

> Think about this for a moment:
>
> A parent on the phone, a child comes home from school running with excitement. He's been shouting "Mummy…mummy…daddy…daddy…". And you know children they can't wait when they are excited, and before he could get his words out,
>
> Parent 1: "Shush"
>
> Parent 2: "What is wrong with you, you are always running into the house?"
>
> Parents 3: "I am busy…just go get your iPad."
>
> Parent 4: "Jade (parent calling to the older child), sort your brother out."
>
> Parent 5: "Why can't you be like your brother and walk quietly into the house?"
>
> What has been your response?

As your baby grows and starts to string words together, you would soon realise whether or not he has a lot to say. Some children have a lot of words and so are ready and eager to share. There are others who may have words to say but keeps to themselves until they deem it appropriate or encouraged. Every child is different and so because your first child has a lot to say does not mean that your second child would too. You must therefore learn to meet each child's level of curiosity in a way that is unique to that child.

For your child who has a lot to say for example, you may encourage them by simply being present, available to them and listening to your child's talk and questions. Sometimes you don't even have to necessarily know the answers to the questions (it's good if you do), they may come out with the answers themselves to educate you when they realise that you are interested in them by giving your time and attention to them. Other times you may suggest that you both go and research (of course depending on the child's age) and agree on a time to meet to further discuss; or research together.

It is a process that you must open yourself to, and be intentional about because it's part of nurturing the gifts in your child. You may even begin to enjoy it too if you give yourself the opportunity. It is your responsibility as a parent to encourage your child to be free in their thoughts and thinking but they require your guidance in the process. So, guide them!

There are many parents who shut down their children even before they begin. Imagine your child run to you with excitement wanting to share with you and your response is, "Be quiet, you talk too much" or "You ask too many questions" "Don't bother me today with your questions and your talk darling." "You are disturbing me; can't you see I'm busy…go to mummy." "Not today, I am busy." The list goes on…it's endless. It may be that you are genuinely tired and busy at that particular time but there are ways to go about that. I say genuinely busy because for some people being on social media chatting and liking things and other people is busy. I mean if you are genuinely busy then explain the situation gently to your child in a manner that they'd understand. Something along the lines of:

"I can see that you want to speak with me and I want to listen to you because you mean so much to me. I also want to give you my full attention so give me 15 minutes to finish this off and I will be all yours."

Seal it with a hug or a rub on the shoulder or a hi five. But you must follow through with what you said you would do.

Otherwise, if your child keeps experiencing this negative attitude and behaviour of you shutting him down, he may withdraw from you since he is "bothering" you. Your child may think that there is something wrong with him or something wrong with being excited about wanting to talk. And so, he may not want to bother any other adult with his questions and talk. Over

> "Train up a child in the way he should go,
> and when he is old, he will not depart from it"

time, it may 'kill' the curiosity nature in him. And you wonder why your child who had so much to say a few months ago now has less or nothing to say.

Asking questions is a good thing. It develops the mind of the child and broadens his or her thinking. A child whose parents are not encouraging his curiosity may find it elsewhere. Can you think of a place? TikTok, Facebook, social media and the internet. Your child may ask Google. Can you see my drift? And these places will engage him or her.

The child who does not have many words or questions also requires your encouragement in a different way to develop his curiosity to the level that is unique to him. He may show his curiosity in the things that he is interested in. And through that you may then engage him and show your interest in whatever he is into. This way you may ask appropriate open questions which may encourage him to explore his thinking and feelings about the thing and share with you in words. For some children it is then they come to light. Not only does your attitude encourage the brain, it is also a way for you to learn something from your child. This can create a good opportunity for you to enjoy your child.

It's a breath of fresh air to learn something from your child and to enjoy your child. Just relax, you don't always have to be rigid, with the "I am the parent...I know it all, I give you the instructions and you follow and I punish you when you do otherwise" attitude. Even if you don't understand or dislike what your child is interested in, it means a lot to your child for you to be interested. It is refreshing to actually get yourself in a place to enjoy something because your child enjoys it.

My son did not speak words or sentences until he was about 4 years old. I was not worried, I mean...the boy took his first steps (walked) at 16 months. Yeah, he took his time. The interesting thing was that he made sounds of things and animals but never used the names. Even he had a sound to call his older sister.

"Train up a child in the way he should go, and when he is old, he will not depart from it"

If you are not careful you may mistake my son for a shy person. When you see him, he is quiet and calm and so he may seem shy but I wouldn't bet on that. He is quiet and calm because he is observant. He takes a lot in. He sees things before I see them or I don't see at all. Not just me…it is the same with others too. He is also endowed with attention to detail. The point is, you may think he does not have many words until you engage him in a conversation involving something that he is interested in.

My son enjoys his games. Yes games. Are you surprised I said games and not some school related subject like Math or Science. Two of his favourites Pokémon and Minecraft. When he is playing these or talking about these, he is on a different level. He tells me every little detail. He could go on for hours. That does not sound like someone who does not have much to say. I encourage him with my attention and I learn a lot from him. I observe his demeanour, I see the light and delight in his eyes as he speaks. It is sheer joy giving him attention and listening to him. He draws me in with his intelligence and knowledge. I have learned the different types of Pokémon such as the Fire, Bug, Flying, Fairy, Fighting, Psychic, Grass, Ground, Ice, Natural, Water, Electric, Dragon, Rock, that is all I can remember. And he quizzes me on them from time to time and we have fun with it.

He suddenly pops up as an orator, a teacher who engages his student (me). This is a gift in my child. Have you given yourself the opportunity to discover what is hidden in your child? What have you discovered? Encourage it and nurture it!

> **A mother once shared with me during a session when I talked about the gifts that children are endowed with but parent destroy them in their formative years. She said that her 4-year-old son sees and says things even before adult around him see them or sometimes they don't see them until he warns them. She tells me that the things he sees and says are true; they are things that may be happening that the person may or may not be aware of. However, whenever he comes out with them, she feels so embarrassed and uncomfortable because he just comes out and says whatever in the presence of person concerned. As**

> "Train up a child in the way he should go,
> and when he is old, he will not depart from it"

an adult and his mother, it puts her in an awkward position. And therefore, her immediate reaction is to shout and scold her son, "Be quiet, you naughty boy. Who told you to be saying things like these, you naughty child."

This child has a gift in its purest form and when he comes out to say the things he sees or the Holy Spirit drops in his spirit, he says them in his innocence. As he is a child, he is not matured and so, he does not know how to be sensitive to the feelings of others when he shares them. He says them as it is; the truth. What I want to make clear is that the mother rebuking and shutting him down by calling him 'naughty' for a good thing (gift) may lead him to eventually withhold and not share it at all. And if this beautiful gift is not nurtured and used to bless others it may die off due to his mother's reactions which are based on fear and anxiety of what others think.

The point to appreciate here is that the child needs guidance in the way and manner he shares his gift with others. Through discussions she realised that her son deserves an apology. I encouraged this mother to apologise to her son for rebuking him for doing good. She may encourage him to share things with her first and then together they may come out with a plan to go about it.

However, ultimately it is the parent's responsibility to seek God's guidance on how to nurture this gift in her son to cause it to grow, blossom and flourish for the good – for the benefit of the boy, his family and others.

I don't know what gift your child may be presenting to you or sharing with you. My question is, do you recognise his gift? Are you nurturing his gift or shutting it down?

"Train up a child in the way he should go, and when he is old, he will not depart from it"

Take a moment to reflect:

How does it make you feel knowing that your child is a good gift?

How would you describe your child? Does your child have a lot of words or has little to say?

How do you engage your child to encourage them?

What have you been doing well and what can you improve?

Having read this chapter, what have you learned and what are you going to do differently if any?

Pray for yourself and your child

"Train up a child in the way he should go,
and when he is old, he will not depart from it"

Chapter 6

Parents

The system is not working. It is not working because we live in broken world. I don't know about you but from my observation, we live in a world which does not always uphold what is good. Sometimes it's as though good is bad and bad is good. Our system is such that bad is not always punished and good is not always rewarded. In other words, doing good does not always get you the reward you were hoping for and so there are people who resort to being dishonest to get them where they want to be.

This state of affairs is creating a lot of confusion around good and evil for a lot of people. And so, many people also end up playing the system thinking that, "What is the point if I am not going to be rewarded for doing good. I will do good when it suits me and bad when it suits me. It's a win-win for me." What does this tell you about our character as a people? Inconsistency and two-faced in character. And more importantly what does this tell you about your own character if you have this kind of attitude? Your child is looking up to you as his or her celebrity, what character are you teaching him or her through your choices, actions and behaviours?

Don't be deceived,

> "Evil doers shall be cut off…" – Psalm 37:9

What they might not realise is that those who choose to do evil and do bad things will be dealt with at the appropriate time. It might not be immediately, but they shall surely be dealt with if they don't amend their ways.

Society is in trouble. Society is in trouble because the communities are in trouble. Communities are in trouble because the family is in shambles. The family is falling apart because mum and dad are in trouble and don't know

> "Train up a child in the way he should go,
> and when he is old, he will not depart from it"

what to do. They are caught up in a confused system. The family is the foundation of society. In fact, the man is the foundation of society. But within this context let consider the family as the foundation of society. Families form community and communities form the society. And therefore, the health of the society is dependent on the health of the family.

And from where I am standing the family is riddled with stress and increasing mental health issues and breakdown in the family system. It is a sad situation and what makes it even more sad is the fact that we are looking for the society system to fix us. The system cannot fix any one, we have to fix ourselves. We've got to start from somewhere. I think starting from the foundation is a good starting point. The family. We can start in our own small way within the family. After all, like I said, the family is the foundation.

I have this to say, when parents start right, choose to be intentional about investing in themselves as individuals and then as parents who prioritise the nurturing of their children as they should, very soon we will see an improvement in the emotional health and spiritual well-being of children. As the family health improves, community health may also improve, and over time, we may have a whole new generation who are emotionally stable and spiritually healthy. Consequently, affecting positively, the health of society. In this way when leaders from this generation who are emotionally and spiritually stable and loved are setting the buttons for the systems of society, they may be loving and sensitive to the needs of the people.

How do we get there?

Parents I appreciate you because you do your best. But if you are only meeting the physical and educational needs of your child, you are neglecting your child in other areas. How about their emotional health, psychological and spiritual needs? These areas usually require a different kind of commitment from you. TIME. And time is something that many parents don't seem to have these days. If you did not know this, now you know that you may be neglecting your child. I was doing my best as a parent but I was ignorant.

Doing my best in ignorance brought me stress, chaos and no peace. And although I thought I was prioritising my children by working to provide for them, I have realised I wasn't at all. I neglected my children until my eyes opened when I was enlightened. I repented and asked for forgiveness. I set myself on a new path to do better to meet those areas that I had neglected for so long. Now I know better, so I do better.

In addition to time, before I could provide and meet those needs, I had to sort myself out in those areas because I couldn't give what I didn't have. It is the same with anyone. No one can give what they don't have. Are you neglecting your child?

Neglected children are not just those under the radar of social services. And if you have been following the story so far, you would agree with me that there are a lot of children neglected in families who are not under social services at all. Today if you child is neglected, you know.

I empathise when I see parents rushed off their feet by a system which makes you feel that if you don't earn a certain amount of money or live a certain life style, you are a NOBODY. And so, people's worth is tied to money and physical possessions. And in some ways, I see why many parents prioritise the physical needs of their children. They think that is what people will see and judge whether or not they are doing well and therefore worthy of friendships and positions among peers and in even in the community.

And therefore, many parents are doing all they can to afford themselves and their children this 'worthiness' characterised by money and possessions. They believe that their child must go to a good school, make good grades to ensure a good job which will pay good money. In the process of acquiring material riches children become pawns. Time for nurturing children is allocated for work outside the home, be it over time or a second job, school homework and attending parents' evenings once a while.

"Train up a child in the way he should go,
and when he is old, he will not depart from it"

Stay at home parents.

In fact, society makes you as a parent feel guilty for choosing to devote your time, full-time to nurture your child at home. You see your neighbours looking at you in a certain way because they don't see you dressed up every morning rushing out with your handbag and laptop dashing for your car. And when they are brave enough to actually ask you, "What do you do for a living?" And you tell them, "I am a full-time mother or father", they look at you like you just dropped from planet Mars. As if something is wrong.

You may even feel embarrassed among your peers because they are all corporately dressed whilst you are in your jog bottoms most of the time during the day. Well, your jog bottoms or whatever clothes you choose to wear are your work clothes just as their suits and ties are theirs. Don't allow yourself to be looked down on. Wear your 'work' clothes with purpose, pride and integrity. People will not afford you the respect if you don't respect your work.

You may feel embarrassed to go out when you are invited into social gatherings because you are worried that your school or college mates might judge you and look down on you for choosing to be a full-time parent. And you find yourself quiet during conversations because you think you have nothing to contribute. And probably some of them may be looking down their noses at you because they are ignorant. But show them you respect yourself; you have character and you are fulfilled in your work of parenting. Share the joys you have nurturing your child. Take pride in your decision to nurture your child full-time and share the 'job satisfaction' you enjoy being a full-time parent. If they are honest, they would tell you they admire you. And those who are dishonest may envy you but fail to admit.

Now let me encourage you, you do such an important job. Don't let society make you feel embarrassed at all. In fact, you work as hard as all of them if not more. Nurturing your child is 24/7 full-time, round the clock life-long work. Just because you don't receive a monthly salary for doing it does not negate the fact that you work hard. It's a career that when done diligently, intentionally and purposefully, you will find fulfilment because it has its own rewards.

It is sad but I have to point it out. Many a times some fathers perceive their wives as worthless and devalue them for being a stay-at-home parent. They look down on them and call them names instead of loving them. And so, some mothers want to go to work outside the home to avoid this and to prove themselves. Come on, you came together and you have produced something beautiful. God has blessed you two with a precious gift (your child). Work together with one vision for your family in love and mutual respect and appreciation for each other's contribution to achieve the vision. Whoever decides to be a stay-at-home parent must be valued and appreciated and loved by the other parent.

Do it onto God

Nurturing children is a great joy but it has challenges. You work hard loving, caring, being kind, compassionate, patient, and being good towards your child. Do it all onto the Lord (Colossians 3:23) and see the reward that finds you. Giving your time to your children is not a waste of time. Who knows, this might be your purpose or calling? This might be the reason for which you were born; to train up your child so that he or she may be a blessing to others. You must do it with all your heart, effort, and soul nurturing and meeting all the needs of your child and see the rewards that flows to you.

I encourage you today that don't allow peer pressure and societal expectations to influence you to drop your three-month-old or six-month-old baby or a year-old baby at a nanny or nursery and run off to work elsewhere, especially when you really don't have to. Only for you to come home tired and neglect the needs of your child. Your child needs you.

I appreciate that there are circumstances that may require some parents to hold down a job in addition to the parenting work. In that case, I am only encouraging you to know the impact of you working another job on your

> "Train up a child in the way he should go,
> and when he is old, he will not depart from it"

child and even on yourself. This way you may not take your day's frustrations on your child when you get home tired and your child is only being a child.

Again, so that you may be intentional about making any little time that you may have with your child meaningful and purposeful in nurturing your child and your relationship.

I am not by any means talking against you going to your job. It is important that you fully examine your motivation for running off to a job especially a second job or choosing to accept an over time, other than allocating that time for your child.

So far I have taken you through some thought provoking discussions, challenging and tough considerations to make as a parent. The coming chapters continue along similar lines hoping to give you information to enable you make informed choices when it comes to parenting your child. I pray that whatever choices you make may be the best for you, your child and your family because you are going to make those decisions with the help of God through the Holy Spirit in Christ Jesus.

"Train up a child in the way he should go, and when he is old, he will not depart from it"

Take a moment to reflect:

Are you meeting your child's emotional and spiritual needs?

How much time do you spend with your child? Is it quality time?

Be honest what was your motivation for going back to work whilst you put your child in a child care facility or nanny or even with family?

Are you a full-time parent? Are you fulfilled or do you look down on yourself?

From what you have learned so far, has your attitude changed and how do you intend to move on in the future.

"Train up a child in the way he should go,
and when he is old, he will not depart from it"

"My secret to parenting is,
I know the Best and I learn from the Best" – Eunice

> "Train up a child in the way he should go, and when he is old, he will not depart from it"

Chapter 7

Be Intentional in your parenting

If you would ask me, staying home to nurture my children would have been my choice, had I known what I know now. Hind sight is a beautiful thing. Having said that, was I in a position to be able to do that? NO! I had to work outside the home. What went against me was the fact that I was not intentional and I cared too much about what others thought or what society would have me think. I was not intentional with nurturing my children because I was ignorant of a lot of things, some of which I have already shared with you.

Enjoy your child

Nurturing your child is already an employment and I hope you would agree with me that it is full-time employment at that. So, don't be embarrassed if nurturing your children is your only employment. And because you want to please others and what society thinks of you or what you to think of yourself, you hurry up to work leaving your 6 month or a year-old baby with nannies and child care centres. I believe it is a good thing to choosing to take on the full-time employment of nurturing your child if you are able to afford. I appreciate that may not be the reality for many families and so parents have to take on work outside the family home. I had to work, go to university, develop a career in addition to nurturing my children. So, I get that.

This is why being intentional becomes so important. You do realise that going to work outside the home can be exhausting and frustrating. And this has nothing to do with your child. It is therefore important that you are intentional not to come home and take your frustration on your child for just being a child. It is not your child's fault that you have to go out there to work.

> "Train up a child in the way he should go,
> and when he is old, he will not depart from it"

And you are certainly not doing your child a favour by going out there to work.

Many parents (me included back then) consciously or unconsciously have an attitude and therefore behave as though they are doing their child a favour when they go out there, work hard to put food on the table and clothes on their backs. You are not doing your child a favour by providing for him or her. It is the same attitude some men have. Some fathers think that paying child support or doing anything for their children is doing the mother a favour. That is wrong. I just thought I would put that out there.

Again, be intentional about the 'spare' time that you may have with your child and make it count. You know that your child is sharing you with your out of home job and so, it is important that you are intentional about the impact of this on your child and minimise it. When you are present with your child, be present and available. Be interested in them and what they have to say or whatever you are doing with them. It can be hard and stressful for you as a parent; however, you want to make the best of the situation without compromising on prioritising your child. And that is why I always say that you need the strength of a supernatural power. Mine is in God because He is my source. He is your source too. Lean on Him.

Your little child does not know neither does he understand that you are tired. He sees mummy or daddy and the next thing you know he just comes running with excitement. This is the time that they talk and talk and talk. You may be thinking, "Oh God, help me, bail me out here." God may not bail you out. You just have to be intentional about this opportunity.

Sometimes when my son has something he wants to talk about and I am in the middle of something usually writing for example. Whenever that happens, I find that I can neither concentrate on what I am doing nor on him because my attention is divided. It messes with me. And if I should stop writing immediately, I may forget my trail of thoughts regarding the point I was making. So, I would say to him, "LD, you are important to me and I love you very much, I want to be able to give you my full attention so could you give me 10minutes to wrap up and I would be all yours." I follow it up by giving him a hug because physical touch is his love language. He understands and accepts that.

I am intentional about getting back to him in the time frame. I can tell you when he starts, he does not stop. I have developed that relationship where he trusts that I would listen and be present with him and be interested in whatever he has to say. He talks about his games with such detail and with excitement. Sometimes, I don't know what he is talking about because I don't play the games with him. They all just go over my head because I don't understand.

But I become thrilled and excited just watching his excitement. He has this light in his eyes and delight in his voice describing the various things that he is doing with the games and talking about those players who cheat on the games whilst playing online. I encourage him by asking questions and showing my interest and with the experience we connect on an intimate level. I am not surprised that I make his best friend list. You can tell that we are enjoying each other. Parenting is not just about taking care of your child. You must enjoy your child.

I have mentioned that my son is 14. I have been intentional about our relationship in the last few years. So, could you imagine the richness of your experience with your child when they get to their teenage years if you become intentional with your relationship as your child is in their formative years and primary school years. And I can tell you that it is priceless. This is your time to build a foundation that may last well into their adult life.

A lady I was mentoring, once came to me with concerns regarding her three-year-old child. She was concerned that her child did not want to settle down when it came to bedtime. He would just cry and cry and cry. On this particular time, we had to cancel the session we had arranged because she had to go walking round the block until her son fell asleep. By the time she was done, she was exhausted and stressed.

"Train up a child in the way he should go,
and when he is old, he will not depart from it"

This lady is a very busy woman, very hard working. She works long hours and does shift work, sometimes working the night shifts. I asked her a few questions to explore the situation and based upon her answers, I suggested a bed time routine that involved her intentional engagement. A couple of weeks later she calls me to tell me that it worked. Her son really enjoys the routine and he is thriving on it. I asked her how she was feeling and her response was the reason why I wanted to share this with you. She says,

"Ma'am, you know how usually I am tired because of work, so it was difficult for me when I first started it. I was not enjoying it at all. But then as I gave myself the opportunity to get into it, I started enjoying myself too. My son can't wait when it is getting to bedtime, he just gets excited to choose the book or story for the night. We read, we sing and we share prayers and we cuddle. Now we both enjoy the bed time routine and I am enjoying my son."

If you read her statement carefully, you will realise that it was difficult for her but she had to allow herself the opportunity to enjoy the routine. Which she did and now has created a good way for them to enjoy each other through the bedtime routine. She is a busy woman who has become intentional at making the little time that she shares with her child count.

Nannies and Childcare

The spiritual and emotional health and wellbeing of your child is important and so you must be intentional about nurturing it. Your protection of your child as a parent should include protecting them emotionally and spiritually. It becomes even more important when you are considering nannies and child care. I had about 4 live-in au-pairs before my son was 2 years old. Then I took him to nursery for child care when he was 2 years old. I was not intentional about any of this. Well…of course I had to research nannies and nurseries to arrive at the ones I chose for my children.

I did physical research. I ignored the emotional and spiritual aspect of the process. There are spirits out there. Spirit can be good or evil. Human beings have spirits in us. And it is sad and also a fact to say that not everyone has a good spirit. Not every person you see have a good spirit dwelling in them. So, you have to be careful. I am talking about this because it is very important.

Look the enemy, Satan does not want good for you nor your child. He wants to destroy the goodness and purity in your child. And he will stop at nothing to do that. Satan roars like a lion seeking who to devour next (1 Peter 5:8). Don't allow him to have you and your child for lunch. So, you must be vigilant and intentional. Your child has no one to protect him spiritually but you. Perhaps you did not have parents who secured you spiritually but you have the opportunity to do that for your child. Grab it with both hands.

Satan is a spirit and he uses human beings to carry out his dirty work. So, if I were you, I would be more careful and intentional when it comes to selecting people to provide child care for your child. No one gave me the heads up on this, but you are blessed that I am sharing this with you. I am not trying to make you paranoid; I am just being real with you.

You cannot see who has a bad spirit with your physical eyes. In fact, majority of us may not be able to tell that someone has a bad spirit. That is why my source – God is so important. Be prayerful and pray over your children. Pray and ask God to lead you to child care providers who have good spirit. And every morning before you leave home cover your child in the blood of Jesus Christ. And if you have to drop him at the nursery or even at school, cover him in the blood of Jesus Christ. Since I have become intentional parent, there is no day that my child leaves home for school that I don't cover him in prayer.

The points that I have discussed here are not just for working parents. They are applicable to every parent. Be Intentional.

"Train up a child in the way he should go,
and when he is old, he will not depart from it"

Take a moment of reflect:

When do you spent meaningful time with your child?

What do you do in those times?

How do you feel and how does your child feel in those moments?

What is the impact on your relationship?

Know what you know so far from this chapter what would you do more off or differently if any?

"Train up a child in the way he should go, and when he is old, he will not depart from it"

Chapter 8
Create opportunity for nurturing

> Do you want your child to grow up and say to his or her friends,
>
> "I speak to my parents but we don't have a relationship."
>
> It's sad, right? How did this happen?

I got it wrong from the start. I think I have said this a few times now. I did not intentionally create opportunities for nurturing my children when they were in their formative years. I did not create opportunities to teach them because I did not know what I was doing. I am not talking about helping them with their homework or teaching them their school work or ABCs. I did that. I remember my little girl told me once that all I was interested in was her school work. That was sad, but I did not realise it at the time, I thought she was talking rubbish. I thought it was funny and so I laughed it off.

What I am referring to here is creating the time and space to teach them about things of life, sharing my personal experience with them. I mean honest and open experience according to their age and maturity. If there was anything I talked about, it was probably to do with how good they had it. I told them they had it good because I provided the things that I was not provided for when I was growing up.

Telling them that they had it good in itself was not bad however the motivation was one of expecting them to be appreciative and respectful to me. It is good for children to appreciate and respect their parents. However,

"Train up a child in the way he should go,
and when he is old, he will not depart from it"

when parents' expectations are such that their behaviours communicate to the children that they owe them, then there is a problem there. I don't know about you but I think that a relationship where one party is made to feel like they owe the other party is not an enjoyable one. It is the same for a parent-child relationship. My daughter once told me, "Mum, I don't owe you." She said it looking right at me and then walked away. Yes, she did. You don't want your child to tell you that when he or she is old enough and brave enough to say the words to your hearing.

I did not create the opportunity to grow and nurture our relationship to make it an enjoyable one. Thinking back, the times that any form of teaching occurred was in the spur of the moment especially when my child had done something I considered wrong or mistake. During those moments, as a parent I was already upset and so the words coming out were commands, instructions and rebuke all of which were delivered with an unpleasant tone:

"Don't do this."

"Don't touch this, it will hurt you. You are a naughty child."

"Come here, you will ruin it."

"I told you the other day to stay away from this, you did not listen."

"I will beat you if you touch this again."

"Stand in the corner and raise your hands"

These are actually not teachings, although many parents may think they are teaching. Some of them are threats. The tone is usually harsh and the voice is raised and so there is no effective teaching if any. What is happening is you instilling fear in your child. That was what I did and when I became intentional, I realised no wonder my child was making the same mistakes over and over again.

> "Train up a child in the way he should go, and when he is old, he will not depart from it"

For some parents the only time they have for their children is when it involves school work. Academic work is good but that shouldn't be your sole focus for your child. Some parents have actually mapped the formal education of their children in detail with its extra-curricular activities also in detail. However, it is sad that there is not intentionality about the detail outline of how to develop the inside of your child – character. Nurturing your child to love himself and love others and be kind and be considerate is nurturing his inside. Nurturing self-discipline in your child will teach him responsibility. I mention these, however it is important that you teach and nurture these characters in them by you being a model for them. You are a celebrity for your child…remember that.

Create opportunities to nurture your relationship regardless of how old your child is. The younger the child the more receptive and open to engaging in nurturing opportunities. I missed out a lot on my daughter because I was not intentional. When I finally became intentional, she was already a teenager and the more I yearned and longed to spend quality time with her, she was unavailable. She was busy doing her own things. I did not create the foundation for it. I have had to work hard to recreate and nurture the relationship between my daughter and I to the peaceful, loving and honest relationship we share and enjoy now. Praise the Lord!

The story is different with my son. My son is much younger than my daughter so he was still pre-teen when I became intentional. I recall from when I used to drop him to school. He was in year six. It was a long drive so I used this opportunity to engage him, teach him a thing or two depending on what comes up in our conversations or something that I had planned to intentionally teach him. I also seized this opportunity to grow our relationship. I was open to him.

He could talk about anything he wanted and I listened and encouraged him. I remember we laughed together, we sung silly songs and made silly faces and laughed some more. I also used this opportunity to teach him the fruits of the spirits and how to live it. I taught him a song that contained the fruits of the

> "Train up a child in the way he should go,
> and when he is old, he will not depart from it"

Spirit so that he could remember them. I also taught him a song that tells him that Jesus loves him. In my own small way, I was nurturing him emotionally and spiritually and strengthening our relationship at the same time.

I had separated from his father at the time and so it was a difficult time for him and for me too. So, I intentionally made this space that we shared together enjoyable and fun. Think about it, we had Monday to Friday on the road and we made it count. We had fun on our school journeys. Now that he is 14 years, we still remember those journeys and we always laugh when we recount some of the things we did. We still sing the songs that I taught him and we enjoy them and whenever I talk about the fruit of the Spirit, he knows them. He can be intentional about them too. It is amazing.

Growing our relationship has enabled my son to be open with me and talk about anything on his mind. I am also open and honest with him and can talk with him about practically anything taking his age and maturity into account. And because I grow our relationship, there is no intimidation or fear of being out of place for my son to ask or share anything. And I mean anything! You are allowed to let your imagination run wild. It's OK. I mean anything. As a teenager, we still create the opportunity for nurturing our relationship, teaching and learning for both of us. It is so fulfilling.

Apart from ad hoc opportunities that may present themselves during the day, we have an intentionally protected time that we talk, connect, share and laugh, sing and play, hug, cuddle and read our Bible and pray. I enjoy my child and allow my child to enjoy me. The 90mins before his bedtime is the time. All screens are off. The TV is off and our phones are put away. That is our time. It is amazing and it is beautiful.

Today count yourself blessed if you have younger children who are in their formative years or even in their pre-teens. If you are in the habit of teaching your child only when you are upset because your child has done something you consider wrong, my advice – change that. Are you yelling and screaming and repeating yourself over and over again? I mean think about it. Are you not tired? Where has that gotten you?

> "Train up a child in the way he should go, and when he is old, he will not depart from it"

I remember it was tiring when I used to do that. It is draining for you and it adds to your child's learning in a negative way. Your child is gradually becoming afraid of you. He may do his best to please you because he is afraid of you. He may eventually lose respect for you. Is that what you want? I have been blessed in my work with the opportunity of meeting with young adults and it is sad when I hear some say, "I speak to my parents but we don't have a relationship." It's sad, right? I don't think you want that to happen to you. It is preventable. My advice:

Create the opportunity to nurture your child and to nurture your relationship.

How do you go about it?

Try having a protected time each day to spend with your child. And make it count. Make it enjoyable. You might consider allowing your child to take the lead sometimes and have fun.

"Train up a child in the way he should go,
and when he is old, he will not depart from it"

Take a moment to reflect:

How do you nurture your relationship?

What have you learned from this chapter that may inform the nurturing of your child, going forward?

Pray for yourself and your child

"Train up a child in the way he should go, and when he is old, he will not depart from it"

Chapter 9
Get yourself ready

I am writing this chapter because many a time when I finish talking about nurturing children, there is a question that always comes through from parents with very young children:

"What is your advice for those of us with very little children?"

In fact, I am writing this book because following the release of my first book, *Parenting Apprenticeship: nurturing teenagers through a new lens,* I was approached many times by parents with younger children to bring out a book to support parents with younger children. I believe that this book will also be of benefit to those who are yet to have children.

Although I am addressing parents with very little children here in this chapter, I am also addressing every parent and parents to be. Parents of infants and babies and toddlers let's talk. Everything that I have talked about so far is for you as well. Remember your child is growing each day and so, your child will get older. Hold dear onto the knowledge whilst your child is growing. You know, God has blessed you because you are strategically placed to get certain things right and in place whilst your child is still very, very little or even yet to be conceived and born.

You are already in the process and so, this is the time to prepare yourself for the miles and miles of the journey ahead. You are at the beginning. My advice to you is sort yourself out. Work on yourself to get yourself ready. If your relationship is not at where it should be with your Creator, God your Father, then be intentional about sorting it out. You must be aware by now that when I talk about your relationship with your God, I am not talking about going to church. Church is good and take it seriously. But what I am talking about is

> "Train up a child in the way he should go,
> and when he is old, he will not depart from it"

your personal relationship with God. He is your Father and He wants a meaningful relationship with you. Probably you are having a difficult time imagining an intimate relationship with Him and so, you are so far away from Him.

You know He is there but you feel you are so far away. You wake up in the morning and you say, "Thank you God for life" and that is it. And when you are going to bed and you remember, you say, "Thank you God for the day, watch over me through the night." And off you sleep. This is not enough. If this is you, you are treating God like an acquaintance. You bump into an acquaintance and you say, "Oh, hello, how are you today?" And on you go. Or at best a casual friend you have a causal relationship with, you may call once a while to check on them just like you check in with God on Sundays when you go to church.

God wants to be a partner and your Father in your life. He wants an intimate relationship with you through, prayer, your reflections and your dealings in your life throughout your day every day. All of it, including nurturing your child. As a Father, not only does He provide for you, He also wants to teach you, guide you, comfort you and give you wisdom in all areas of your life. Like I said in an earlier chapter, this may happen when you cultivate, a meaningful and intimate relationship with Him.

For the sake of your child, do it. This is your opportunity to grow your relationship with your Father. Become committed and learn from Him to nurture your child through your relationship with Him. Whilst you are sorting your relationship out, allow the Holy Spirit to work on you. Learn to know yourself as a person. Learn to discover yourself as a person and cultivate a relationship with yourself. Your relationship with yourself is the foundation upon which all other relationships including the one between you and your child are built.

I tell you; you must sort your character out. Work on your character by creating boundaries based on love. Create boundaries that communicate love to you. This creation of boundaries from love for yourself, is what will then become the foundation for setting boundaries for your little child. **Boundaries** are for protection and love. We will explore boundaries in the chapters to follow shortly.

Decide on areas that you want to grow. You may use the fruit of the Spirit (Galatians 5:22-23) to help you. Let me remind you again that you are a celebrity to your child. What character do you want to model for your child? You may start from there. For example, you may want your child to be honest or grow to be a person of integrity. Ask yourself, "am I honest, am I a person of integrity?" Set boundaries to discipline yourself to grow in that area. Setting boundaries in this area is loving yourself and loving others. As honest person and a person of integrity, you are reliable and trustworthy. This brings you self-respect and you earn the respect of others by blessing them with the fruit of your integrity. It sounds good, right?

The way I would go about this would be to give myself a score of where I am at the moment when it comes to being honest. So, on a scale of 1 to 10, 1 being the worst and 10 being the best give yourself a score. Then work from there. When I say honesty, I mean honesty. Not honesty tainted with so-called white lies. Of course, if you want your child to tell you white lies then … Your child may grow up to have their own definition of white lies which may not conform or agree with your definition. What then? I will leave that for you to decide.

When it comes to being honest for me, I remove even the white lies. I count the white lies as lies. So, I may come out with the boundary to tell the truth no matter what. Be honest even when no one is watching. I mean when no human eyes are watching. The fact is, God is always watching and that actually is pretty amazing knowledge because I love God I choose to stay within the boundary.

Of course, I am human and I may slip from time to time, but when I do, I recognise and don't excuse it by saying, "No one is perfect". I don't beat myself up either. I acknowledge it and ask for forgiveness and I continue on the journey of honesty. And because I have the Holy Spirit with me, He reminds me the next time I encounter a situation that requires me to be honest. Little by little like growing a muscle, I grow stronger and stronger in telling the truth no matter what. I can tell you; I now do a pretty good job.

As a parent you require lots of patience. Not only that, as a parent you would want your child to be patient. How can you teach your child patience if you are not patient yourself? This is your opportunity to grow your patience. Formulate boundaries based on love that may nurture and grow the muscle of patience in you. In our world today where everything is rushed. We are encouraged to think on our feet for anything and everything; this is definitely a muscle to grow. Be different ...move away from what society is teaching you to what God your Father is teaching you. PATIENCE is one of the fruits of the spirits.

This is what I would do. It is always good to keep the words of the boundary positive. This helps you to develop positive vocabulary for yourself, for your child, for your family and for your home. The following will serve the purpose of boundaries geared at exercising patience.

1. I will give myself the opportunity to think before I respond.

2. I will give myself the opportunity to think through things

3. I will give myself the opportunity to calm down

4. I will give myself the opportunity to respond rather than react

5. I will give myself the opportunity to hear others out

6. All the above requires me to take a deep breath, pause and ...wait!

7. I will give myself the opportunity to maintain a healthy blood pressure and heart rate by being calm

8. I am loving myself by being patient

9. I am loving others by being patient

10. I am loving God by being patient

11. **I will give myself the opportunity to pray and wait on God. NOW THAT'S BEING PATIENT.**

Let's look at LOVE itself. Let's talk about the setting boundaries on LOVE. As a parent you are endowed to love unconditionally. Maybe you don't know that yet. Maybe you don't know that you are capable of loving unconditionally. Well, you are because you are created in the image of God. God commands you to love unconditionally because He has given you the capacity and ability to do so. The only way you may love unconditionally is by seeing through God's eyes. To put it in another way, it is important that you are connected to God.

At the moment, your little prince or princess may be at a stage where he or she can barely open their eyes or they make you smile or they make you laugh with their funny and pure gestures. Do yourself a favour and do your child a favour…get yourself ready. At the moment that you have fallen so much in love with your little one is the time to get yourself ready. Get yourself ready so that you are not taken by surprise. Get yourself ready and gather some nuggets for the journey. Get yourself ready to be in position. Get yourself ready to align yourself. Get yourself ready to build a solid foundation. Get yourself ready because…

A time is coming when your little prince's or princess's behaviour may begin to irritate you and give you a run for your money. A time is coming when they may challenge you in ways that you never thought could be possible. A time is coming when the foundation you build now will be tested against all odds. Will the foundation stand? Will you stand?

*"Train up a child in the way he should go,
and when he is old, he will not depart from it"*

Ask yourself the question, "Will I still be in love with my prince or princess? Or my love would be measured in doses based on their behaviour and response to me?"

This is the time to grow the muscle of unconditional love now that your little child can barely string 2 words together. Your child needs you to love him or her unconditionally regardless of his or her behaviour. Your child needs your love regardless of what he or she does or does not do. Therefore, you must learn to love your child because you are his or her mother or father. Love them because she or he is your child. Love him or her because… just because…

To be able to love in that manner, you must yourself:

- **See through God's eyes to appreciate His love for you.**
- **See your worth through God's eyes**
- **See who you are through God's eyes**
- **See yourself beautiful through God's eyes**
- **See yourself accepted through God's eyes**
- **See yourself amazing through God's eyes**
- **See yourself capable through God's eyes**
- **See yourself loved by God no matter what.**
- **Accept and transfer God's love for you to love yourself not based on your behaviour because God loves you unconditionally. There is nothing you can ever do to change God's mind from loving you.**

When you have been able to do this, you are setting yourself the foundation to love your child unconditionally because your confidence from loving your child is from God. Your confidence for loving your child is based on the fact that you see through God's eyes. When you love your child the way you ought to love them, you will be good to them and love them right, no matter what.

So now that we are clear on loving yourself and loving your child, let's consider the following as boundaries for LOVE. In no particular order:

1. I will see myself through God's eyes

2. I am worthy to be loved

3. I am confident in knowing that God loves me

4. I love myself not based on what I do or don't do. I love myself because God loves me

5. I will extend the same grace to others – my child being number one after my spouse.

6. I will look up to God whilst I am growing this muscle.

I have given you some examples around boundaries based on the foundation of love dealing with being honest and patient and love itself. These are just to start you off. Be creative. You may explore other areas of your character and set boundaries for them. Always remember,

Boundaries are protection and love for life.

Ground yourself in your character. This is so good because these are the sort of things you would be passing onto your child by modelling it out for them. So here is your cue:

Get yourself prepared...Get yourself ready...

Let me share a word of prayer with you:

Our Heavenly Father,

"Train up a child in the way he should go,
and when he is old, he will not depart from it"

I thank You for the opportunity to share what You have taught me with anyone readying this book. I pray that You enable them to start well. I pray You help them to build solid foundation based on Your Love when they are setting boundaries based on love. Help those who started wrongly to make a U-turn to fortify the foundations. Always remind them of Your crown of lovingkindness and tender mercies. In name of Jesus Christ of Nazareth.

Amen!

"Train up a child in the way he should go, and when he is old, he will not depart from it"

Take a moment to reflect:

From what you have read from this chapter, in what ways have you learned to get yourself ready for your child?

What boundaries rooted in love are you going to set to discipline yourself whilst you prepare yourself for your child?

Pray for yourself and your child.

"Train up a child in the way he should go, and when he is old, he will not depart from it"

Chapter 10
Behaviour Management

When my children were younger, I did behaviour management. That was what I was advised by health professionals to do in order to control behaviour of my children. Don't be surprised, I was a health professional who also taught parents and families to do behaviour management as part of their parenting.

I put measures in place so that when my children went out of line according to what I believed or perceived to be out of line or wrong, that they'd receive punishments. Behaviour management in simple terms is if a child behaves badly, he or she received a punishment decided by the parent in the hope that the child will be deterred from engaging in that behaviour in future.

In this case you as the parent becomes, the controller and your child, the controlled. In essence, in your bid to change your child or make sure your child behaves in a good manner, you control your child through the punishments you give to him or her.

I remember one of my usual behavioural management punishments I used was time-out. Time-out in itself is good when used appropriately as a love boundary and not as punishment (I will talk about this in a little while). I used time-out on the stairs or in the corner or facing the wall, and sometimes with hands raised. I know others send their child to their room in their frustration.

And whenever my children were having a time-out, they could be in the corner or on the stairs for God knows how long. There was no strategy or planning to it. I was angry they'd misbehaved and so in the heat of the moment, I would send them to corner or stairs, which ever appealed to me at the time.

"Train up a child in the way he should go,
and when he is old, he will not depart from it"

Let me point this out, as children growing up, they are expected to make mistakes and that was something I did not quite grasp with its implications. And so, when they made mistakes especially around the same thing, I became frustrated because I felt the punishment was not working. Why are they not responding to the punishment? My next plan of action will be to intensify it.

Without even realising it, I set out to manipulate them further. Sometimes I sent them to the corner with their hands raised and also turned off the light. I allowed them to stay in the darkness to manipulate or control them to change and behave better – whatever that was. My children are good from birth but because I did not understand how to nurture the goodness in them, I bought into the idea that I had to manage behaviour through punishment (which I thought were boundaries by the way) to bring out the goodness in them. I was wrong.

I was wrong because I had the wrong idea. With the wrong idea came wrong strategy. Ultimately, I had good intentions to bring the goodness in them but my approach was focused on using deterrent to stop bad behaviour. This is a negative approach. It is negative parenting. It is unfulfilling; its stressful; and very frustrating. You feel drained and unappreciated and your child feels unloved.

I have learned that if you want the goodness out of something, you feed it with goodness. I know it seems simple enough but it is not easy to do when you have been programmed to think that you must stop your child from misbehaving at all cost. Let me break it down.

Take for example, you buy a plant for home. You know the potential of the plant. You want the plant to grow and blossom, flourish and bear fruit (good fruits), if it is a fruit bearing plant – its full potential. So, what do you do? You feed it with good stuff – good soil, good compost, good sunlight, good water to enable the plant achieve its full potential. Along the way if something were to go wrong, you would not insult the plant or decide to deprive it of water for example. You would still continue to feed the plant with good stuff it needs. It is the same with your child when you are nurturing the goodness in your child.

When you keep feeding negative energy to something which is supposed to be positive, eventually the negative will overshadow the positive and the result will be negative. If you feed positive energy to something negative, the positive will eventually overcome the negative and the result will be positive. Paul the Apostle puts it beautifully in Romans 12:21

"Do not be overcome by evil, but overcome evil with good."

It means be good and do good even when things seem bad; and you will overcome. This is not you being in denial. But this is you saying, "I choose to see beyond the negative behaviour. I see goodness in you, I see your potential and so I will nurture the goodness. I will feed you with good things."

Thank God I learned differently and those lessons have changed things around for me in a peaceful and fulfilling way. I am delighted that I have the opportunity to share with you especially as you have a young child.

You may be treading on the same path of behaviour management just as I did. How is that going for you? Or you may be on your way to the path of behaviour management, then beware. You don't want your child to look at you one day and tell you that you were mean with all those behaviour management punishments. And that he or she felt unloved. It broke my heart when my 11-year-old son was brave enough to tell me after years of behaviour management. I felt horrible and I thanked God for the new path of love boundaries.

Let me share with you want I learned. I am sure I have said this before but I would like to say it again. No one can change anyone and certainly human beings are not created to be controlled by one another. No human should dominate another regardless of their age or relationship. You may try to control someone including your child. It may seem as though you are

> "Train up a child in the way he should go,
> and when he is old, he will not depart from it"

succeeding and you may believe that, until one day, they become brave enough to rebel. And they will.

You have your free will to choose and your child has his or her free will to choose too. And right from day one you must recognise this and nurture your child to be able to freely exercise their will to choose in freedom – without you controlling or manipulating them to do what you want. But you say, "My child does not know right from wrong." And that is true, and you must teach him or her that. But before you can teach what is rightly right and rightly wrong, you must know that for yourself.

And many parents think they know what is right for their children but they actually don't. Many parents' knowledge and understanding of what is right and wrong is rooted in fears. Fears of failure, fears of what others think… just fears.

So how do you nurture your child to choose in freedom? This is what I have learned and I live by. I learned the boundary of choosing in freedom and I live by that boundary and I teach that to my children. This is what I recommend:

1) Teach your child to love himself, love others and be considerate. Let your child know that they can do whatever they want but not everything is beneficial (1 Corinthians 6:12). Once your child is able to understand this with its implications, he is then in a position to weigh his choice from the competing alternatives on the scale of beneficial and unbeneficial. It is easier and your child may learn if you live by this same standard. Remember you are your child's celebrity.

2) Set love boundaries that allow him to freely exercise his freedom to choose based on loving himself, loving others and being considerate.

This should be at the core of nurturing the goodness in your child through love boundaries rather than punishments. I am not saying that your child will not go through the consequences of their actions and choice. Of course, he would. What I am emphasising here is your focus should not be on the punishment but the benefits of choosing right – which is loving himself, loving others and being considerate. Throughout your child's stages of growth and development this should grow and develop with him or her. You start little and you build on it.

You buy your five-year-old a toy. You sit your child down and explain the boundaries of the toy to your child so that they understand. This must be based on love. You may say something along these lines,

"I know you will love this toy and that is why I bought it for you. I know you will be happy when you play with it and so you must look after it. When you finish playing with it, you must put it in the drawer. This way your toy is taken care off. And as long as you look after it you may play with it and enjoy yourself. If you don't put it back in the drawer when you finish playing with it, it may damage or you might lose it. And you may not get another one. And that will make you sad. I don't want you to be sad because it will make me sad too. Do you want to be sad?" I can hear that little voice saying, "No mummy, I don't want to be sad." You may conclude, "I want you to be happy and you want to be happy so take care of it and enjoy it. I love you." And then follow it through with his or her love language – hug for example.

So, you have given your child the free will to choose to love herself by taking care of her toy in order to continue to enjoy playing with it; and also, to love you in the process as well by protecting your investment. She may also choose otherwise (not to care for her toy) and in that case the natural consequences are already in place – damage to toy or lost toy which will make her sad and not get another one.

In this love boundary your child is learning that she is responsible for protecting her happiness and loving herself. It is her choice.

And therefore, there is no need for you to be angry and shout at your child if she makes a choice not to put the toy in the drawer and can't find it. If she

> "Train up a child in the way he should go,
> and when he is old, he will not depart from it"

comes to you crying and upset, this is not the time for you to shout at her or send her in the corner to spend time there because you feel she disobeyed you. No, she made a choice; you just don't like her choice. She has to learn from it with your support in the right way. And she will if you give her the opportunity to.

Yours is to respect your child's choice and love them regardless; allow her to talk it through, if she wants to; empathise with her for being sad whilst you allow the consequence for her choice to happen naturally. In this case, she loses the privilege of playing with the toy because it is lost. And yes, she may be sad, but she will feel your love. This is powerful.

Sometimes parents feel that when their child misbehaves and they show him love or hug him, it means they are encouraging the bad behaviour. That is what I used to think too. But no, that's not true. You rebuke the bad behaviour, but the love is for your child regardless of the behaviour. And that's why my son tells me that I am considerate, kind and loving even when he makes mistakes or choses to do wrong things. He says we have love boundaries and we talk through things and he likes that. It makes him feel loved.

And because of this, his character is developing and growing in an amazing way which tells in his behaviour through his choices. He loves himself, loves others and considerate in his choices. And we live in peace and we are joyful in our relationship.

When setting boundaries, consider these:

- Take into consideration your child's age, development and understanding. Every child is different. You know your child better than anyone.
- Make them simple around everyday things. Start with one or two things and as he grows in this area and also grow in understanding, you may add others. But please don't set out to control everything.

- Don't overwhelm your child. As he grows in discipline in one area it may extend to other areas.
- It's a process so be patient with yourself and your child. Children make wrong choices and mistakes; lots of them. It comes with the territory. They also learn in a nurturing environment and with your support. To be fair we all make mistakes and wrong choices for being human and the fact that life is a learning process.
- Don't allow Satan to manipulate you to think that because you have made some terrible mistakes and choices in your own life, you want to prevent your child at all cost from making same mistakes as you. And so, you allow fear to cripple you to act in a way that will steal, kill and destroy your peace and joy in your relationship with your child. You are a celebrity to your child but your child is not you. Instead of being fearful, be prayerful.
- This is not a quick fix. It is about growing the goodness in your child from the inside to manifest outside in your child's choices and through his or her behaviours. It takes time so please don't be in a hurry otherwise you may miss the whole point of it. Enjoy the little everyday progress. Recognise them and celebrate them. For your five-old who puts her toy away in the drawer, recognise it and celebrate her. This will encourage her to keep it up. Keep encouraging her as she gets older, even when she annoys you. It's like water for a plant. We are quick to judge and criticise bad behaviour but we overlook recognition and celebration for good stuff. Your recognition, and celebration is water to her good choice of loving herself and you.

I believe that this is a good way to invest in a good foundation to setting boundaries even for the teenage years and later in life. Even for your child to also teach his or her children. What a blessing! What a legacy!

> "Train up a child in the way he should go,
> and when he is old, he will not depart from it"

And even if you have some challenges in the teenage years, because you already have a grounded foundation, your child will always come back to that foundation. That is what the Bible teaches us in Proverbs 22:6:

"Train up a child the way he should go and when he is old, he will not depart from it."

I started moving away from behaviour management to love boundaries when my son was 9 years old and my daughter was a teenager. It was a difficult task. I call it 'too late syndrome'. It does not mean it's too late, it just means the situation requires more work. First, to uproot the wrong foundation, prepare the ground before new seeds can be planted and nurtured for growth – new foundation. It takes more time, more energy, more effort, more commitment; more everything. I was determined and so I walked through the fire (too late syndrome) with dedication and the help of God. And here I am telling you the story.

Before I end this chapter, let me take this opportunity to say something little about time-out as I said earlier I would. Time-out may be incorporated into love boundaries. It can be good for both parent and child to nurture patience and peace which will grow love in your relationship. Time-out is good when you want to give yourself the opportunity and your child the opportunity to think through something that has happened between your child and yourself. It may be used when your child is able to understand the implications that taking time out is actually to think through what has happened as you the parent do the same. Then at an agreed time limit, that you have predetermined, both of you will come together to share your thoughts on the matter and to resolve it in love.

It creates respect as you both listen to each other air out their feelings and thoughts and it does not matter whether the parent think the child is wrong, it is important that the child is given the opportunity to be heard. Then come to a common ground to move forward. And usually where apologies are due, it gives the opportunity to do that in a loving and thoughtful manner because you have had time to process the situation. Parents can say sorry to their child regardless of how old your child is if you believe you over reacted. Your child will appreciate that and learn from you.

I believe time-out can be a useful tool but it must be used appropriately to benefit the relationship. It can even be used between husbands and wives and in any other relationship to help deal with conflicts and misunderstandings to grow the relationship.

You are so blessed. You have a much, much younger child. Take the opportunity now.

Say *bye* to behaviour management and…

Hello to love boundaries.

God bless. Love is patient Love is kind

"Train up a child in the way he should go,
and when he is old, he will not depart from it"

Take a moment to reflect:

Are you doing behaviour management? How is it going for you?

If you have been using time-out, reflect on your use of it in relation to the result you have achieved so far.

What have you learned from this chapter that you did not know before? How will this impact your parenting now and for the future?

Pray for yourself and your child.

"Train up a child in the way he should go, and when he is old, he will not depart from it"

Chapter 11
Love Boundaries.

I wouldn't say reading is my favourite thing. But I have cultivated the habit of reading because, it is important. **I see it as investing in myself**. I don't know about you, but if you don't like reading, I suggest you start to cultivate the habit of reading. One day you would want your child to read so you start reading now to grow the discipline of reading so that your child may copy you. If you enjoy reading then this is up your ally; you may find this easier. Not just reading anything by the way, but reading things that add value to your life.

I read things that will add meaning to my life. Materials that I can learn valuable lessons so that I can grow and flourish. Since I became intentional about nurturing my children and not just parenting any-how, the Holy Spirit directs me to materials and resources that supports my journey.

I know many people who say they do not like to read but they spend their time reading posts from social media and things that do not add value to their lives. They like the gossips. When it comes to things that actually matter, they are of the opinion that reading is not something they like or enjoy. "It's boring," they say. My question then is how do you learn and grow when you despise the materials that will enable you to do so?

Don't get me wrong, I was once not into reading too. I had abandoned reading for many years until when things got tough for me and I realised that things had to change in my life. That was when I started reading and researching. This was later 2016 and I have never stopped. I am also blessed to be a fast learner and whenever I want to apply knowledge that I have been blessed with, I do not make excuses or waste time, I just get on and do it. I

> "Train up a child in the way he should go,
> and when he is old, he will not depart from it"

also commit myself into the hands of the Holy Spirit guidance. You don't have to be a fast learner; you just have to be committed.

I make mistakes or sometimes I forget but then because I have made up my mind to learn, I am conscious of it, and I am prompted by the Holy Spirit when I forget or make a mistake. So, I dust myself and try again, I continue in the process until I get it. I do not make excuses for myself but I persevere with a learning heart and attitude. I will encourage you to cultivate the habit of reading and a learning heart if indeed you really want to be nurtured to nurture on your journey of parenting. As a parent of a young child, as I have already put across, you are blessed to position yourself before your child becomes a teenager.

I learned something from one of the books I read not long ago. I learned something about setting boundaries and I am going to share this with. After reading the book I have drawn the conclusion that when I set boundaries, I will have 3 things in mind: mange myself, love, and give choice to my children. The relationship between myself and my children has its foundation on love. So, when it comes to setting boundaries, it is important that it protects the relationship.

What is boundary. A boundary according to the Compact Oxford English Dictionary for Students is "a line marking the limits of an area or a limit especially of a subject or area of activity." From this we can deduce that a boundary shows the demarcation within which it is safe to operate. Therefore, boundaries are supposed to protect your child and your relationship. And protective boundaries are rooted in love, not fear and not intimidation. That is why I call them love boundaries.

There are some boundaries that actually tear down your child and your relationship with your child. Your intention may not be to tear down your child but that is what might happen if your boundaries are not truly rooted in love. I have learned to set boundaries that protect the relationship with my children. That is what I am sharing with you. It is very important to learn and accept the fact that you are only able to control yourself in any relationship including the relationship with your children. You cannot control or change anyone.

When I am setting boundaries, I have learned to manage myself in love, and give my children choice in love in order to protect our relationship. Love does not force or control people or others. Love does not manipulate or coerce or intimidate people to do things they do not want to do. Love is patient. Love is kind. Love gives the choice to choose what you want to do.

In managing myself I have learned to control myself by not losing my cool even when my buttons are pushed or I don't like what my child is choosing to do. I ground myself by setting out to do what I want to do in the situation. I communicate what I will do in the situation clearly to my child and I do just that. I make sure that I follow through with what I said I will do, so that there is consistency. This communicates respect and trust to my children because I am doing exactly what I said I will do. They may resist and throw an emotional fit but they eventually get the message that I am doing exactly what I said I will do.

Let just say taking showers and my son are not best friends. I am sure a lot of boys and even men are not best friends with showers or taking their baths. Don't shoot me if you are a man reading this, I am just saying what I have observed. Despite the fact that there are quite many men and boys who find showers and taking their baths as a chore does not make it normal. It is rather a common issue because you may be experiencing it in your home too. Or you might know someone in that situation.

My son and I discussed boundaries around showers. He was old enough to understand the implications. My son decided when he wanted to shower, we agreed, and he got on with it. I have learned not to take it personally or force or control him about that. In fact, we play around with it.

One day however when I collected him from school after his sports day at school, his legs were covered in dirt. So, I asked him, "Are you going to have

"Train up a child in the way he should go,
and when he is old, he will not depart from it"

your shower today?" "No mum" was his response. I continued, "Your legs are pretty dirty and whether you have your shower or not is entirely up to you. But this is what I am going to do. I will not allow you to sit on the sofa without having your shower because I do not want dirt on the sofa." You can imagine the emotional fit, "No that's not fair, I am not having my shower". I just looked at him and expressed my empathy for his predicament with "Oh poor LD, I get it". I call him LD sometimes.

He didn't have to have his shower, although I would like for him to. And I was not going to make him. He however had a decision to make for himself.

Then we got home. He came to the kitchen and helped himself to an ice lolly from the freezer. We have an open plan kitchen and living area so I saw what he was up to when he came to the kitchen for as I was sitting in the living room. He left the kitchen. After about 10mins I called him for something and I asked where he was, he told me he was sitting on the stairs eating his ice lolly. I said OK. I told him I was going to make his dinner for him. I had even forgotten about our conversation about the sofa and the shower. It was after another 5 minutes I called him to asked him something and he said to me he was going to have his shower and it all came to me. Then I remembered our conversation. I smiled with satisfaction and said thank you Lord.

He showered and came to relax at his usual spot on the sofa and watch his favourite television programmes. How refreshing? Calm relaxed atmosphere. PEACEFUL. I gave him the choice to do what he wanted and the consequence of his action was clear to him. You can do it too. It is important that you remain calm and control your own actions and not your child's.

I will give you another example. My son and I had agreed that in the morning when I am dropping him to school, he will not be on his phone so that we could have good conversation about the day ahead and anything that we wanted to talk about. One morning when I was dropping him off, we arrived at the station earlier on this day as he was taking the train to school. As we were waiting in the car, he went on his phone playing a game.

When I saw that, I said to him "I can see that you are on your phone, you can continue to do that if that is what you want to do. However, this is what I will do: I am happy to wait here with you but not while you are on your phone." As soon as I finished my sentence, the car door opened and he run out to the train station upset. "I love you and God bless you, have a blessed day" as the words came out of my mouth just chasing after him as he run off.

In this situation he had a decision to make because he had two options before him. Each option with its own consequence. He could choose to stay on his phone but I will be gone, or he could choose to put the phone away and he may enjoy my company. I kept my composure and calmness the whole time. I did not become angry with him because he went on his phone. I did not give him a lecture to make him come off his phone. I did not raise my voice in any way. I gave him his choice in love and I communicated with him what I was going to do in love and I managed myself in the situation. Let me share with you what happened.

Barely 3 minutes later, my phone rang. It was him. I thought to myself, "Has his train been cancelled?" As soon as I answered the phone, I heard the words, "I am sorry mama" in such a humble and sorry tone. My heart just melted and I felt that God is good. I responded, "I love you LD and I forgive you. God bless you and look after you. You know that God has given you all the goodness in you. And that makes you a good person. You have the choice to live this goodness that God has blessed you with." I tell him this every morning when I bless him before school. "Yes mama, I know, and I love you too. Bye mama".

This is love, this is respect and this is trust. This is managing myself in love, giving my son his freedom to choose in love and protecting our relationship in love. It is such stress-free, meaningful and fulfilling. It is peaceful and joyful and hopeful.

You can do it too. As soon as your child is able to understand simple things in a meaningful way, just set boundaries around everyday things to love and

"Train up a child in the way he should go,
and when he is old, he will not depart from it"

protect your child and your relationship. The idea is love and not control or punishment. Don't overwhelm your child with lots of boundaries especially when they are little. Don't be overly protective trying to control everything. One or two at a time. Make them easy and simple to understand and let it be clear for both of you. Set it before hand with your child. And usually, the consequence is inherent in the boundary as you can see from my examples above. Remember to keep your cool and manage yourself and allow your child the choice.

Give it a go. Try it.

"Train up a child in the way he should go, and when he is old, he will not depart from it"

Take a moment to reflect:

Do you read? If so, what do you read?

Based on what you have learned from this chapter, are you going to make changes to your reading habits? If so, what?

Do you have boundaries at home for yourself and your child? If so are they love boundaries?

From what you have learned reading this chapter, what will you do differently about setting boundaries, if any?

Pray for yourself and your child

*"Train up a child in the way he should go,
and when he is old, he will not depart from it"*

Chapter 12
Nurtured to Nurture

I was speaking with my mother the other day. She was telling me how men these days want to marry women who work out of the home to earn a living. They look for professional women. That is the trend now. Why? In our society today, the man cannot financially provide for the family on his income alone and so that is the solution they have come up with. And this is the state of affairs now because the economy is challenging and the financial crisis is immense. With the man working away from home and his professional wife to-be working away from home, I wonder if he's given any thoughts to who is going nurture the children and how the children are going to be nurtured in a nurturing environment? Some men expect their professional wives to take this on as well as supporting the family financially, and this has created a lot of tension and chaos in many homes.

Right from the get go, you are conditioned to prioritise provision and so you look at finances, how to pay the bills, rent, food, clothes and other provisions for the family. So, it is not a surprise that for many homes, mum and dad both work outside the home.

For some they have their focus on a certain level of lifestyle. Their attitudes and behaviours centre on working to pay for that big house, ride in the latest car, wear those designer clothes, put their children in the private schools and pay for the range of extracurricular activities, the going on several holidays a year and live the "I have arrived life."

And so, you run off to work leaving your child at home by themselves or with the house help or au-pair or childcare facilities to take care of them.

"Train up a child in the way he should go,
and when he is old, he will not depart from it"

I used to run off to work doing the 2 jobs and overtimes until I realised that I may lose my children. Until the Holy Spirit opened me up to realise that I was destroying my children.

You are more important than the house.

You are more important than the food on the table.

You are more important than the clothes you wear.

You are more important than that car.

You being a parent and parenting your child goes beyond providing food, clothes, and best schools.

I am not against parents working, I have said this before in an earlier chapter. But the motivations for working; the reasons for running off to your job and the impact it is having on your life and that of your child is what I am drawing your attention to.

I will tell you what happened to me. When I was running off to my job to pay bills and provisions, I was stressed, exhausted and frustrated, unappreciated and things between my husband and I was a mess. I was diagnosed with an auto immune condition because I was just under such stress. The arguments at home were something else. I call them verbal battles. I called the police on my own child one day because I couldn't deal with this 'alien' in my home. I mean the 'alien' that the parents had created.

Then I submitted myself to parenting apprenticeship and allowed myself to be nurtured to nurture. And that was what I was missing all along. That set me on the right path to the peace and joy I enjoy in my life today. I learned the truth and that truth set me free. I dedicated myself to nurturing my children for God and with God. I became confident and resolved.

Allowing myself to be nurtured to nurture is the best thing that ever happened to me. I won't go back to the way I used to live. Oh, please God, don't let me go back. My life is amazing. I enjoy my life. In fact, the other day I looked at myself in the mirror and said to myself in my heart, "I love my life, thank you God." By the time I realised the words were just coming out of my mouth.

Don't get me wrong. You might think I have no problems. Well, I am not immune to problems as long as we have life, problems are inevitable. So, I do have my own challenges in my life just like anyone else but I find myself walking through challenge after challenge, test after test with such strength and ability, and confidence and joy. It so peaceful and amazing all because I allowed myself to be nurtured and live and walk in the lessons and teachings with wisdom every day. It is so true when God promises to be with you in Psalms 143:1-3:

"Fear not, for I have redeemed you; I have called you by your name; you are mine. When you pass through the waters, I will be with you; and through the rivers, they shall not overflow you. When you walk through the fire, you shall not be burned, Nor shall the flame scorch you. For I am the Lord your God."

When you have such revelation and receive it into your innermost being, you exhume with confidence that propels you along no matter what because you know God is with you.

It did not happen by chance. I started by asking myself some difficult questions when things became chaotic and confusion plagued my home. I asked

"Is this what life's all about?"

"Who is nurturing my children?"

"Who am I learning from?"

And that put me on the path of being hungry for change. And so, I set out to satisfy this hunger. And the more I looked and researched the hungrier I

> "Train up a child in the way he should go,
> and when he is old, he will not depart from it"

became. In the process I discovered who I am and that changed everything. I became dangerous. Dangerously good. I mean I found myself and I realised that all of my life I had been ignorant, what I sometimes call 'sleep-walking' – living anyhow with no meaning, leaning on my own understanding, allowing tradition, custom, culture and other distortions to blind me.

I repented and I allowed the Holy Spirit in to connect me to my God who created me in His image and likeness, who is also my Father – The KING. And that means I am a princess!

The Holy Spirit teaches and guides me into all truth – the truth about who I am; the truth about my parenting and how to do it; and the truth about how to live life in fulfilment. The truth about how to function in the way God created me to function. And you would be amazed, when I forget He reminds me.

God knows how you are supposed to function because He made you. In essence you are His product and He is the Manufacturer. And so, if you want to know how to function you go to the Manufacturer. You have to tap into the mind or connect to the mind of the Manufacturer either directly or through the manual.

When I became aware that I had malfunctioned for a long time, and to reverse the malfunctioning, I couldn't do it myself. I had to reconnect to my Manufacturer – God. I could only do that through His Holy Spirit. I call Him my Supervisor that God has given to humanity to teach and guide so that we may function according to how we were meant to be. Through Him I function and have life. The Spirit of God has ignited life to all the areas of my life that were dead when I was 'sleep-walking'. How did the death occur? Satan came to steal, to kill and to destroy. That is how. But Jesus Christ came that we may have life and have it abundantly (John 10:10).

I am awake! I am alive and I feel alive since the last 6 years. I feel like I am now 6 years old. I look forward to life, to parenting, to working in the purpose for which I was created with delight and peace looking up to God through His Holy Spirit.

I am grateful for the privilege to share this with you. And you are one blessed celebrity parent. I had to crack this for myself. I had no one to tell me about the things I tell you today. God allowed me to go through it; hit rock bottom; go through the process to figure things out for myself for a reason. Why? To tell you. To share with you. That you can choose differently. And as He was there to walk me through and He is still walking me through that He'd do the same with you if you would allow yourself to be nurtured to nurture.

I know that it may not be that simple to make a shift from where you find yourself at the moment. You need a revelation. I had a revelation and so I pray for a revelation for you as a parent of a young child in the name of Jesus Christ of Nazareth, so that you may allow yourself to be nurtured to nurture. God bless.

"Train up a child in the way he should go,
and when he is old, he will not depart from it"

Heavenly Father,

I thank you for today. Thank you for anyone reading this book. I believe it is not by chance that they find themselves reading this. I remember when I was looking for material and researching to change for the better; that you directed me to appropriate resources that moved me from a state of 'sleep-walking' to a state of being awake and alive in you.

I pray that even as they read you may grant them the spirit of your wisdom. I pray for the revelation of the knowledge of God to enlighten them and to open their understanding in all areas of their lives including nurturing their children. Move them from a state of 'sleep-walking' to a state of awakening in you. This I ask in the name of Jesus Christ of Nazareth.

Amen!

"Train up a child in the way he should go,
and when he is old, he will not depart from it"

Take a moment to reflect:

In your own words, what have you learned from this chapter?

Pray for yourself and your child

"Train up a child in the way he should go, and when he is old, he will not depart from it"

Chapter 13
Wisdom

For as long as I can remember I have been taught to learn to earn a living. When I was a young girl growing up, the focus was learning hard which will ensure that I get a good paying job. The emphasis is even huge today as parents and children alike have been and are being programmed to place education above anything else in life if not the only thing. Society including parents are parenting our children in a way that will make them 'successful'. And our definition of success is making the top grades, going to Russel group university or Ivy league university and earning a good living from a good paying job. I have observed that education is programmed in such a manner that is tunnelled visioned – to be employed.

I just want to put this out there. You are therefore in trouble if at the end of it all, you don't find a job. Your life becomes meaningless and you become frustrated and angry about life and with everyone. Many people in developing countries find themselves in this predicament of frustration and anger because they did what they were told to do but they didn't get what they had been learning for; the reward; the job. They blame the government for their unemployment and joblessness and dissatisfaction.

We educate our children to earn a living. Is that what life is about? We live to earn a living. And then what? I will tell you what…we mess up in life. We have jobs but we are miserable and stressed. We have top paying jobs but we are depressed. We earn lots of money but some cheat others for that. Why? Because whilst our parents were busily educating us children for a job, they didn't nurture us about life. They didn't nurture us about character; how to handle life; and how to live life itself.

And so, we fail miserably in other areas of life as we've grown up and become adults. We fail in our relationships with ourselves as individuals and our

> "Train up a child in the way he should go,
> and when he is old, he will not depart from it"

relationships with others. We fail at home and we fail at our marriages. Take a look at broken homes and the divorce rates. We have become brilliant failures. I don't know about you but that is what I have observed in our world today among adults. And the sad thing is we the adults are guiding our children along the same path – brilliant failures.

We have so much information thrown at us. At a click of a button, swipe of a screen, press on a button you name it, you have access to tons and tons of information and so why is life so stressful and confusing and chaotic. Why is there no peace in our homes? We have not been taught and so have not learned how to build and maintain peaceful homes.

Our children are so confused and depressed in life. Why? Because they do not know who they are or why they are and so their very essence and foundation is threatened. Sexuality confusions, suicidal thoughts and ideations, mental health problems plague our children.

Today as a parent of a child reading this book, I challenge you to think differently. I challenge you to change the story for your child and your child's children. I challenge you to have a different attitude. I challenge you to take a new look through a new lens of nurturing.

Whilst your child is still little and growing, teach him or her about life and how to live life. Do this right from day one or now according to their age and understanding. You might not know how yourself yet, but with a learning heart and being intentional about learning, you are off to a good start. I am sure that by now, having read this far on in this book, I want to believe that you have picked up some tools; some knowledge of wisdom. May I take this opportunity to remind you that as a celebrity to your child, you are his or her first contact and example of information about life and how to live life and handle life. This leads me to a very important point – Wisdom.

Be a wise parent. When I talk about wise parent, I don't mean street-wise as some people call it or human wisdom. I am referring to supernatural wisdom that comes from God through His Holy Spirit lowered to our human understanding. Human wisdom can only take you so far because it lacks depth and cannot see the whole picture. It may follow logic and miss the hidden meaning. It highlights the problems and may not present any true solutions or hope for the problems.

That is why training up a child in the way he should go must not be based on your human wisdom but the knowledge and wisdom of God. This wisdom enables you to understand and act in a godly manner to nurture your child even when human mind cannot understand. To obtain the God kind of wisdom is by fearing Him. Solomon puts it perfectly when he says in Proverbs 9:10

"The fear of the Lord is the beginning of wisdom."

Fear here does not mean to be afraid of God because He will hurt you or anything like that. But it is the respect, reverence and obedience you give to Him for being who He Is – Almighty God, who is also your Father. As a wise Parent:

- Ask for wisdom from God to nurture your child (God's child), in the way he should go to fulfil his Godly purpose in his life just like Solomon asked for wisdom from God to enable him rule God's people, Israel. God was delighted that Solomon did not ask for riches and wealth for himself. God blessed him with His wisdom and wealth, riches and fame became added bonus. God will be delighted with your request and He will grant it to you as James confidently highlights, "If any one lacks wisdom, let him ask of God, who gives to all liberally and without reproach, and it will be given to him." – James 1:5.
- God knows that you need His wisdom to succeed and because your success is His success and He glorifies you for His name's sake.
- Be intentional about how you live your life as a parent, both you and your spouse. The choices you make and why you make them must be done consciously knowing that they also impact on your child and

- the fact that he or she may be copying you has to be taken into account. I want my teenager to read books that adds value to his life. As well as telling him and encouraging him to read, I decided to read such books myself.
- What are your values and beliefs and your standards. Define them clearly for yourself and be discipline about them so that they may be clearly seen in your daily living. It becomes easy to teach them to your children when you live by them. I have learned to value love – unconditional love and I intentionally learned to love my children regardless of what they do or don't do. I have learned to see beyond behaviour to who they are through God's eyes and so I love them unconditionally. It was not easy for me at first because it was difficult to love when your child behaviour is so far away from your mark but through God's wisdom, I have come a long way and it is so peaceful. You can too.
- Choose to live an honest and a grateful life and impart these virtues to your child by matching your words to your actions in everyday things of life and at home. Be honest in words but kind when it involves rebuke or corrections either towards your child or your spouse. Grow an honest relationship between you and your spouse in a respectful appreciative manner, and valuing one another. Listening to one another and being considerate are ways to communicate respect and valuing one another.
- Be affectionate with your words and gestures towards your spouse in the presence of your child. Do I sense, "Eww" coming from you? But Why Not? If you can argue in the presence of your child without a second thought, how come you feel uncomfortable or hesitant with doing something that is good (showing affection) which may have a positive impact on your child in the presence of your child?
- Recognise the people in your life, the things in your life and be grateful to God for these blessings and be content whilst you work towards becoming the best, the leader that God created you to be.
- Go easy on the academic work. Share your life with your children and create the environment that encourages discussions and

conversations on all areas of life including relationships and sex. Yes, Sex. If you don't, your child will find out from elsewhere. I can think of a few, can you? School, friends, social media… These sources should not be the first reference guide for your child.

First things first

There are many things competing for our attention. Different attractive alternatives vying for our attention. There are so many important things that we have on our lists. You have yours and I have mine. We have to be able to organise all these important things in order of priority. And as a parent of a young child, set the priority for your success and your child's success. How do you know what the priority is? Look no further, the answer is in the manual of life:

> "But first seek the kingdom of God and His righteousness and all things shall be added on to you." – Matthew 6:33

When the people of Jesus' days were busying themselves working for what they will eat and drink and wear; when they were busily stressing themselves working for a living and living unfulfilled lives, Jesus drew their attention to what they were doing wrong – wrong priority. In their human eyes, they were to work for their food and provision, but Jesus says that is not how God created us. Our bodies and lives are worth more to God than food, drinks and clothes. God did not create us to toil for these things because He knows we need them and as a King, He provides these to his children. And so, Jesus reminds us of the priority of God for us which comprises 2 factors:

1. Seek first the kingdom of God (his will, purpose, intention, character, nature)

2. His righteousness (right standing with God: align yourself to be positioned properly with God)

> "Train up a child in the way he should go,
> and when he is old, he will not depart from it"

Achieving these 2 factors which form the priority of God for us will unlock the other things that we need in life without us toiling or working for those things. It is simple but our human mind struggles to comprehend. It's like buy one, get one free promotion. To get the free item you must buy one first. The priority is first buying one and then another one is added to you for free. You cannot have the free item without first buying one. You may try to get the free item without first buying one, but that will be stressful, unfulfilling and you may end up behind bars because you may attempt to steal. There is no way around it, you must buy one to have the free item.

You need the revelation and the wisdom of God to fully grasp this in order to succeed. And that is why your friendship with the Holy Spirit is so important because He teaches and enables you to navigate through these things successfully. Once you are able to do that for yourself, you teach your child.

Society and your up-bringing have trained you to educate your child for a job to earn a living and for many years that has been your priority – working for money. You might be wondering, "So I don't have to work." Yes, you will work but you don't work for money. Your priority and motivation for working is serving your gifts and talents to bless humanity to propagate the Kingdom of God.

Today, you have learned a new priority which does not involve working for food or bills or clothes. A priority that must be fulfilled to grant you access to daily things of life that you need, without toiling for them. You are your child's celebrity.

And so today, I encourage you to ask God for WISDOM.

"Train up a child in the way he should go, and when he is old, he will not depart from it"

Take a moment to reflect:

Cast your mind back to your childhood, what was your experience when in relation to education or going to school?

What is your aim for educating your child? Has it changed after reading this?

What is your priority for your life?

What is your priority for your child?

Going forward: What would you do more off or differently after reading this piece?

Pray for yourself and your child.

"Train up a child in the way he should go,
and when he is old, he will not depart from it"

"The secret to peace and joy in your parenting journey lies in Holy Spirit directed parenting – it always has and it always will."

– Eunice Essien

> "Train up a child in the way he should go,
> and when he is old, he will not depart from it"

I appreciate you

Thank you for buying and taking the time to read my book, I hope you have enjoyed reading it as much as I did writing it. Have you learned a thing or two?

I look forward to sharing with you again in the future. In the meantime, you may want to check out my other book, *Parenting Apprenticeship: nurturing teenagers through a new lens.*

God   bless

"Train up a child in the way he should go, and when he is old, he will not depart from it"

About Author.

"Once a nurse always a nurse." Eunice, is a trained paediatric nurse and a Specialist Community Public Health Nurse (health visitor), who worked with children and their families in the hospitals and in the community in the UK for many years.

Eunice is still a nurse, but a different kind of nurse working to bring healing and peace to children and their families in the church and in the community and the world at large. She does it through Parenting. Parenting is her thing. It's her story. She is privileged and blessed with two children, a young adult and a teenager who are testimonies because God uses them to give her so much insight and understanding and wisdom to share. Nurturing children, teenagers and young adults has become her thing.

She had a revelation and then learned to become what she calls, a committed parent apprentice, enjoying peace joy and hope on this journey. And it is her passion, conviction and vision to bring the light to others. She says, "I know the Best and I learn from the Best."

She is honest, kind and has a good sense of humour. She enjoys having a good laugh. She adores spending time with herself, her family and her friends.

ANOTHER BOOK FROM THE AUTHOR

www.ingramcontent.com/pod-product-compliance
Lightning Source LLC
Chambersburg PA
CBHW041145110526
44590CB00027B/4136